Betty Blythe

Style Me Vintage

A guide to hosting perfect vintage tea events

tea parties

Lulu Gwynne opened Betty Blythe vintage tea rooms and fine food pantry in West London in 2008. Staffed with pretty girls in vintage outfits and red lipstick, Betty Blythe is a service-based establishment, serving up delectable afternoon teas to discerning clientele. Lulu specialises in tea party experiences for children, hen parties, or indeed anyone wishing to indulge in a vintage experience. As well as devouring delectable cakes and pastries, visitors can delve into her vintage dressing up box and take lessons in etiquette in beautiful surroundings, reviving age-old tea traditions.

Find her at: www.bettyblythe.co.uk

Betty Blythe was one of Hollywood's earliest sex symbols. Born Elizabeth Blythe Slaughter in Los Angeles, she appeared on Broadway and the London stage before making her film debut in 1918. Two years later she signed with Fox Films as a replacement for screen vamp Theda Bara and became a popular matinée idol in costume epics and dramas with high society settings. A voluptuous brunette, she was known for her skimpy costumes. Her biggest hit was *The Queen of Sheba* (1921), but, with the exception of *She* (1925), all her major silent films are considered lost, with only still photography remaining as evidence of their censorship-challenging raciness.

Betty Blythe

Style Me Vintage

A guide to hosting perfect vintage events

tea parties

PAVILION

With very good wish
Betty Blythe

Contents

Introduction

Make every day a holiday and celebrate life; tea parties, birthday parties, dinner parties, cocktail parties, Christmas parties, street parties, bridal showers, baby showers, costume parties, surprise parties, engagements, fundraisers, graduations, weddings, stag nights, hen nights, pre-parties, after-parties… seriously, life can be one big party!

I love throwing parties – and life at Betty Blythe is often like one big social occasion! I meet so many lovely people and I never tire of the thrilled faces of guests as they arrive to their table set for tea, or the excitement of little girls preparing for a dressing-up tea party! You may be planning your first party or becoming the chief party planner of your social group. Some of us are good at throwing parties and some like playing the part of guest. Whichever type of party person you are, use this book as a source of inspiration to create vintage-style gatherings for the people you like having around you. It has been lovingly written to help you organise a vintage tea party from scratch, with advice from my party-planning experiences.

To help you on your vintage journey, I bring to each chapter a party suggestion for each era: a classic Victorian tea party, an Edwardian breakfast, a 1920's speakeasy, an elegant 1930's soirée, a 1940's picnic and a 1950's street party. There are notes on how to celebrate each particular event, but you may see fit to alter the suggestions to your personal requirements and tastes. I suggest how to set the scene, where to hold the party and how to style it using easily obtainable vintage crockery and props. There are tips on what music to listen to and helpful "how-to" guides. Each party theme also comes with an achievable menu of recipes inspired by that era's popular foods. You can recreate them or have some fun inventing your own.

In our fast-paced world, we can get so busy that we don't really spend quality time with others. Hospitality is a much-needed gift to lift the spirit – this can be a gift we give to our families, our neighbours, parents of our children's friends, or colleagues, as well as a gift to our close friends; friendships are built on shared memories, so start creating some fantastic memories by planning a party with a vintage infusion!

With every good wish

♡ lulu

"Enjoy the little things, for one day you may look back and realise they were the big things."

About Lulu Gwynne

The dress was ankle-length, with pink roses on the front, my hair curled over my shoulders and my new shoes were being shown off – everything was ready for the party. The tea table was set, the decorations were up and the entertainers had arrived – I was ready to greet my guests. It was my 4th birthday party. This day left a great impression on me and I love remembering all the specialness that my parents had so thoughtfully brought together – it was a truly lovely day. I had wished for a cake, seen in the local bakery window, the one where a sponge cake had been dressed as a Sindy. I can still see the front door, through which so many people I loved and who loved me came, bearing beautifully wrapped gifts. I can remember the taste of jam sandwiches on white bread, nibbling off the colourful topping from an iced party biscuit, and putting Hula Hoop crisps on the end of every finger before eating them. Pass the parcel, pin the tail on the donkey, music and dancing and bubbles in the air…

From that magical day on, I have always made it my unofficial role to take any new situation and make a party of it! From gathering all the children of the village regularly in one place and having such a wonderful time we called it Fun Club, to party organiser throughout college and university. I am still amazed that the bars and venues accommodated wild and carefree and pretty drunk students dressed as cowgirls and spacemen and a bus filled with James Bonds and his girls, but what brilliant nights they were!

From urban street festivals, to fashion shows, to promotional nights, fundraisers, weddings, christenings and the most sophisticated of soirées, thirty years on from my most memorable party I feel so privileged to be part of the lives of people on their most important occasions. It's a party for me every day of the year and I wouldn't have it any other way!

About Betty Blythe

Fabulous food, quintessential Englishness and a hint of Hollywood glamour all served up on a vintage platter is what makes the Betty Blythe Vintage Tea Room experience unique. When setting up the café (in Blythe Road) I needed a name. In a moment of serendipity the name Betty Blythe came to me, along with a feeling of familiarity, and when I discovered that Betty Blythe existed as an actual person I felt an instant tingle of confidence. This beautiful icon of the silent movie era has watched over us as we serve our wonderful customers, and we have paid tribute to her costumes by dressing as starlets ourselves and accessorising the guests too as they take tea at Betty Blythe. As an acquantaince of Betty's once commented: "I think Betty would consider it a real hoot that someone named a business after her."

It is a wonderful experience to hear the excitement build as the dressing up box is opened, as the previously mild manners of the party turn to shrieks of laugher, and the guests start posing in the array of hats, faux fur stoles, pearls and gloves I keep in the box. This goes on until each guest is satisfied with the finished look.

It is then time for tea and mismatched sets of china adorn the tables with white tablecloths and scattered petals. A pretty flower display will be placed in the centre of the table and pots of tea are brought to the guests. A selection of fine sandwiches, scones and cakes is brought to tempt the guests until they are pleasantly replete!

How to organise a successful party

The beginning

I like to begin with a beautiful new notebook to get me started on any party or new project. In it, I write down all the ideas that have kept me awake at night – and I try to reflect back on them when doing my research and buying. Of course, part of the reward of the experience is the journey along the way – ask any bride who has organised her wedding. We live in a wonderful world where the internet can solve even the most extraordinary of requests, but it is good to keep yourself in check – write down your budget (and try to stick to it), plan and schedule your styling, but also make a note of all the new contacts and leads you discover along the way (you never know when you might need them again).

Most importantly, be flexible. Realise from the start that not everything will go as planned (in most cases, you will be the only one to know that).

"The difference between try and triumph is a little umph!"

Venue

Get the location right and this can allow you to smoothly set the scene. This could be as simple as planning to clear your garden and tend to the grass, or may involve a visit to venues to view a hotel, country house or bar space. When you are considering location, you will want to keep in mind the following:

- Room capacity – how many people does it comfortably allow? (Also: how many guests will you have – you may harbour ambitions of hundreds of guests turning up, but one thing I have learnt is that you can't guarantee a full turn out – people have the most amazing excuses on the night – so consider scaling down a bit.) Choose smaller and more intimate spaces for less formal gatherings, especially evening events, as the atmosphere will be cold if there are massive spaces between each guest.
- Check with the venue managers what you can and can't do, e.g., do they have they a late licence so your guests can drink well into the night, do they permit dancing, do they have a dance floor, can they accommodate entertainers and their equipment? Check access for large equipment and see how many flights of stairs you have to plan for! What other things can they help you with? What are the hire costs and are they reasonable to your budget?
- Think about lighting. You may visit in the day, so remember to picture it at night. Subtle lighting is nice for dinner parties – can you use candlelight? For extra dramatic lighting, you may need to call in an equipment hire company.
- Location. Does it have good parking? Is it easy to find? Make sure you give good instructions on how to get there or your phone will be ringing non-stop with frustrated party guests just as you are trying to welcome others. Note the nearest transport links and offer numbers for a taxi company able to collect your weary guests at the end of a night's partying.

Invitations

Creating and sending invitations is one of the most enjoyable parts of the party planning process. That little golden ticket to your fabulous event is the first step in displaying to your guests what the party has to entice them. Make sure you spell out every detail. Think who, why, when, where, and what to wear...

Food and drink

Taking on the food and drink is a big responsibility. It may take many days of preparation and will always take longer than you think. Unless you are confident that you can do the food preparations as well as everything else that needs to be done, this is best delegated to friends who make cooking look easy, or catering companies. If you are hiring a venue, they will most usually be able to offer something to suit and many food stores now offer take-out party food. The recipes I have suggested in this book are easy to prepare and take the hassle out of having to devise a menu, but think ahead about what you can manage.

Have you somewhere to chill the drinks? Remember to empty out fridges at home, as it does not look great to stash bottles between open packets of food and last night's takeaway. Have the ice delivered if needed, or pick up a readymade bag from the supermarket or local store, and get something to use as an ice bucket. You guests will appreciate this thought – a chilled drink with ice is so much more sophisticated. No one wants warm champagne! Do not forget to set the drinks chilling a few hours before the party starts.

How to serve Champagne:

Champagne is synonymous with success, celebration, and good times, but how do you open it without attracting too much attention and look good doing so?

- Chill the bottle, for about three hours in the refrigerator or half an hour in a bucket of ice water. Fizz corks are rather potent when the contents are not cold enough and can shoot out unexpectedly.
- Wrap a towel or cloth around the bottle, to guard against the unlikely event of breakage.
- Remove the foil wrapper.
- Place one hand firmly on the neck of the bottle, with your thumb maintaining pressure on the metal cage against the cork.
- Twist to remove the wire cage and shift your thumb to maintain pressure on the cork, in case the pressure of the contents tries to pop the cork prematurely. Sometimes a surprise pop can happen, so always be very careful where you are pointing – I have a few dents in ceilings I can name.
- Tilt the bottle at a 45° angle, facing away from you.
- Holding the cork firmly, slowly twist the bottle. Remember: turn the bottle, not the cork.
- As you feel the cork begin to loosen and rise, maintain pressure with your hand. Allow the cork to slowly ease out of the bottle. If done correctly, you will hear a gentle "sigh" rather than a "pop" (although, just for fun, a pop can be very satisfying...).
- Hold the bottle by its base. Place your thumb into its deep punt (the concave in the base) and cradle the bottle in your other four fingers.
- Pour a small amount in each champagne glass. As the initial foam subsides, pour more Champagne into each glass. Never fill to the top – leave space for it to settle.
- If pouring many glasses, one will always fizz over and catch you out – you can discreetly place your finger on the rim to stop it, so it doesn't drip on people's clothes.
- Enjoy, as the bubbles carry your guests through a fabulous evening…

Vintage themes

If you have a passion for a certain era, indulge yourself completely. Start with the design of the invitations, think about the choice of venue, stock up on the inexhaustible amount of decorations and props. Dressing up in appropriate attire can take an outing all of its own! Thinking about all of these details will make a party all the more fun and entertaining for your guests and unforgettable for the right reasons.

Sourcing vintage

My passion for vintage clothes and crockery began whilst I was still earning pocket money. The first treasure I ever fell in love with cost me 50p and was a rainbow-coloured diamond-effect round brooch. This was when my inner magpie was released. I knew that looking within the little baskets on jumble sale stalls was where something beautiful was waiting to be discovered. I grew up in a town where charity shops continued to reveal the most amazing vintage finds: Edwardian salt and pepper sets, Art Deco jewellery, 1950's clothing… I spent many a happy weekend being drawn to vintage crockery on the market stalls and antique shops. In fact (so my mum used to joke), I was the only 13 year old who didn't just have a bottom drawer (a young woman's collection of housewares to bring to a marriage), I had a bottom cupboard! You can imagine how much I'd accumulated by the time I came to open Betty Blythe. I needed somewhere for it all to go, so a vintage tea room was probably the only solution!

Well, golly, more and more people are selling vintage clothes and china these days, so while it is a little easier to source the really unique pieces that can add such a personal touch to your party, it is going to cost you money. There is a healthy market for vintage and its modern reproductions but there are still many original treasures to be found. Add to your adventures by rummaging in the places others wouldn't think to look.

- First, you have to always be looking! Discuss it with anyone you meet and always mention you are looking for vintage items. You never know who you might meet who has an attic, kitchen or wardrobe full of old things.

- Another way to source is to scour all of your local antique stores. Leave your information if you are looking for something in particular.

- Keep up to date on auctions in your area. Although some auctions really drive up the prices of vintage, once in a while you can find one where you walk away with a few good deals.

- In the summer, visit as many car boot and garage sales as possible! Take cash and be ready to pay what you think you want to pay for it. If you fall in love with something you just have to buy it, I say!

- Visit charity shops and house clearance warehouses. It's hard to find desirable vintage items there these days, but sometimes you will find a gem and they are usually reasonably priced.

- The internet can be a great place so plan some time to spend on this and be mindful to keep looking for the best prices rather than immediately pressing the buy button. This is the easiest place to blow your budget without thinking clearly! Be era-accurate in your searches too.

Invitation Etiquette

If you are lucky enough to be invited to an event, be it a wedding, a dinner party or an afternoon tea party, this invitation comes with some important obligations:

What does RSVP mean?
From the French, it means *"répondez, s'il vous plaît,"* or "please reply." This is a polite way of the hosts asking you to reply and let them know if you are attending. It is better to reply promptly, within a day or two of receiving an invitation, so that the host can make her plans. Arrangements are made in anticipation of how many people are attending (food and drink, table settings, etc.), so please be thoughtful of this.

How do I respond?
Reply in the manner indicated on the invitation.
- RSVP and no response card: a handwritten response to the host at the return address on the envelope using your own stationary or pretty card.
- Response card: fill in and reply by the date indicated and return in the enclosed envelope.
- RSVP with phone number: telephone and make sure to speak in person – answering machines can be unreliable.
- RSVP with email: you may accept or decline electronically.
- Regrets only: reply only if you cannot attend. If your host doesn't hear from you, tables will be set in anticipation of your presence.
- No reply requested? Unusual, but it is always polite to let someone know your intentions. A phone call would be sufficient.

Is that your final answer?

Changing a "yes" to a "no" is only acceptable on account of: illness or injury, a death in the family or an unavoidable professional or business conflict. Call your hosts immediately.

Cancelling because you have a "better" offer or not showing up is unacceptable and you may experience not being invited to further events.

Changing a "no" to a "yes" is good news to the host who invited you, as they wished for your company in the first instance, but do give good notice of your intentions and hope it won't upset the host's plans.

"May I bring…?"

Don't even ask! An invitation is extended to those the hosts want to invite – and no one else.
…a date. Some invitations indicate that you may invite a guest or date (Miss M Bennett and Guest) and when you reply, you should indicate whether you are bringing someone, and give their name.
…my children. If they were invited, the invitation would have said so.

Say "Thank You."

Make sure to thank your hosts before you leave, and then again by phone or note the next day.

Party Planning Essential Checklist

Let's get this party started!
- Choose the occasion you are celebrating and what date you are proposing.
- Keep it personal and make it special for those you wish to be there.
- Establish your party budget. How much can you spend?
- Ask people to bring their own drinks if you supplied the food.
- Complete your guest list and create a list with contact details.
- Find and reserve venue if having the party away from home.
- Select the party theme and research some ideas.
- If you are having your food catered, find and hire a caterer.
- Create and send party invitations.
- Manage RSVP by checking off the list and keep tabs on contact numbers.

You can never plan enough
- Write out an hourly plan of the party and what needs to be done.
- Don't forget the next day for putting things back together, returning items.
- Have a Plan B for weather changes.
- Plan your party menu and make a shopping list.
- Check for food intolerances amongst your guests and any special requirements.
- Decide on what décor, backdrops and decorations you wish to have, and purchase them.
- Decide on music – your own compilations and play list made in advance, a band or a DJ?
- Plan an entertainer or party games in advance.
- Plan more games than you need, in case one doesn't quite fit the mood.
- Order any party rental props or electrical equipment.
- Purchase non-perishable food and drink.
- If you are hosting your party away from home or hiring a caterer, call to confirm bookings.
- Check on non-RSVPing guests so you can make food for the right numbers.
- Make sure your camera is ready to be used for the party.

- Make checklists of all the little details, so you can remind yourself on the day.
- Order a bespoke cake in advance.
- Order flower arrangements.

The day before
- Enlist the help of close friends for the preparations.
- Confirm with location and caterer again.
- Refrigerate drinks.
- Make provisions for soft drinks, otherwise it is rather time consuming hunting for that lost bottle of sparkling elderflower!
- Prepare food that can be refrigerated, make sauces, wash and chop vegetables.
- Decorate and arrange your home for the party – think of the safety of others.
- Clean your house. Put out clean towels. Make sure you have enough toilet paper.
- Try on your outfit – it will be too late on the day if something is wrong with it!
- Have your mobile phone charged up – it may be a busy few days for usage!

On the party day
- Get up nice and early and try to work to a schedule, to make the day go smoothly.
- Set up tables and bar – don't forget tablecloths.
- Arrange tables and chairs so they are spread around, giving options to sit or stand – you can't rearrange when people are sat comfortably.
- Think about the first impressions – is the room tidy, clear and easy to navigate?
- Prepare food and keep refrigerated until ready to serve – be mindful of food safety.
- Chill wine and other drinks.
- Remember to pick up that cake or flowers you ordered.
- Get out all the glasses and lay them in rows – check for chips or grubby glasses.
- Pick up ice and have it ready in buckets. Put down floor protective sheets in case of leaks.

- Get dressed in advance, at least an hour before the party starts.
- Light candles and start music.
- Clear away evidence of packaging – and start with an empty rubbish bin.
- Keep your mobile phone at hand, as someone always needs directions.
- Put keys and personal belongings in a safe place.

During the party

- Make sure that drinks are readily available on arrival. Your guests will be keen to feel comfortable and a drink in the hand will achieve this nicely.
- Have champagne/soft drinks poured and waiting on a tray if this is what you've planned.
- Give guests specific jobs to warm the party up – it makes them feel involved and gives them good reason to start conversation, taking coats, offering drinks, monitoring the music.
- Keep an eye on levels of food and drink and keep it flowing! Have others hand around food, so that you can concentrate on keeping the party flowing.
- A good host keeps an eye out for things like spillages and floor hazards. Let your party be talked about for the right reasons, not an emergency tale.
- Keep an eye on the lighting and make it in keeping with the time of day, dim down for later in the evening.
- Listen for the music and keep it appropriate to mood. Try to not let it lapse/switch off, as it can spoil the moment.
- Look back at your checklist to remind yourself of what needs to be done – you will be busy but you are still in charge of the experience for others.
- Keep the mood going – the invitations gave a good indication of the party theme and you are responsible for maintaining the atmosphere. Make an effort – the small details and personal experiences will keep your guests talking about your party for ever more.
- Hire a photographer or take pictures to capture the wonderful moments forever.

End of the party

- If all things have gone well, the food will eaten and enjoyed, the drinks will be drunk and a memorable time will have been had by all. The party will come to a natural close.
- If you have to make it clear that it's time to leave, turn the music off and bring up the lights. Thank people for coming and offer to get their coats as a polite way of moving on stragglers.
- Are you giving your guests little favours as they leave? Make more than you think you will need, just in case.

The next day

- Possibly an early start if contract hire companies are coming to collect their equipment.
- Be available on your phone or to answer the door.
- Return back to the venue to pick up and dismantle the decorations from the night before.
- Take boxes and black bags with you to clear up.
- Recycle your empty bottles and glasses.
- Return to friends anything you may have borrowed.
- Leave venues as you found them – if not better.
- Account for breakages or losses. Be careful with hire companies and count everything back in.
- Don't forget the thank you notes! This is one of the most overlooked, but most important, party planning tips. Thank you notes also let the guests know that they were an important part of your event. Send pictures you have from the night for a personal touch.
- Finally, sit back and have a well-deserved cup of tea!

Victorian Tea Party

There's just something so feminine, sophisticated and elegant about hosting a Victorian-style high tea with delicious treats and impeccable manners. Tea parties can be a lovely time for mothers and daughters, baby showers and hen parties – but you don't really need a reason to have a tea party – it is just the perfect way to spend time with your friends. Indulge yourself by slowing down the pace of life for a while, savouring the delicious goodies and catching up on gossip.

For a touch of true vintage etiquette, send handwritten cards or ready-made invitations. Invite your guests for one o'clock or three o'clock and encourage them to dress up with "appropriate attire" (no one expects a crinoline these days, but it's nicer if everyone makes an effort rather than turning up in jeans).

Betty Blythe has her own menu for this afternoon tea experience. It is simple, but offers enough variety for even the most picky eaters and will make your guests pleasantly replete and happy.

MENU

A selection of Finger Sandwiches
on white crustless bread:
Cool Cucumber; Smoked Salmon,
Dill and Cream Cheese;
Roast Beef and Watercress

Mini Mixed Fruit Tartlets

Homemade Mini Cherry Scones
served with Raspberry and Rose Jam
and Devonshire Clotted Cream

Victoria Sponge with
Fresh Strawberries and Cream

Chocolate Marble Cake

Setting the scene

Afternoon tea is a typically British experience. Prior to the introduction of tea into Britain, the English had two main meals – breakfast and dinner. Breakfast consisted of ale, bread and beef. Dinner was a massive, long meal at the end of the day. It was no wonder that Anna, the Duchess of Bedford experienced a "sinking feeling" in the late afternoon. Adopting the European tea service format, she invited friends to join her for an additional afternoon meal at five o'clock in her rooms at Belvoir Castle. The menu centred around small cakes, bread and butter sandwiches, assorted sweets, and, of course, tea. The tea menu was made in the kitchen and carried to the boudoir of lady of the house who waited with her invited guests, surrounded by fine porcelain from China. Food and tea was then passed among the guests, while they enjoyed conversation.

Your own home is the perfect place to hold a tea party. Once the ladies' boudoir was the most usual setting, or out on the lawn, but the only requisites are table and chairs. Use the dining room table if you can, or a low-level coffee table surrounded with comfortable seating, or a patio table and garden chairs if you are going *al fresco*.

Collect together your vintage crockery in the weeks leading up to your event. You may have some already, but lovely things can be found at markets, car boot sales and charity shops. Don't worry about it all matching – that's the genuine appeal of the whole look. If you don't want to buy, there are many crockery hire companies who can provide complete sets and small businesses on the internet have some real gems. There are plenty of people willing to sell their secondhand treasures, but don't spend a lot of money on the china. Be careful to look for hairline cracks on the handles – you want to drink the tea, not wear it on your silk vintage dresses.

How to lay out the table

The size of your party (and table!) will determine if you present the tea on a sideboard for guests to help themselves or whether you can arrange it in the centre of the table itself.

One must have a pretty tablecloth hanging a least a foot off the edge of the table. Markets and charity shops always have embroidered or lace vintage tablecloths, so go and rummage for a great bargain. If you prefer a modern tablecloth, look for pretty floral or good plain linen ones.

A large teapot is the main item. If you use loose tea you will need a tea strainer too – find one that has its own holder or it will stain your tablecloth. Practice with your tea pot beforehand – it may look beautiful, but pour terribly – you don't want a fuss.

Other items you will need for the table setting:
- teacups and saucers: one for every guest and a few spare
- teaspoons for each saucer
- a small cake plate placed in front of each chair or sitting, with the cup and saucer to the top right of the plate
- small napkins, placed on the right side of the plate
- a dainty knife or cake fork for each person, placed on top of the napkin
- a bowl of white sugar lumps with sugar tongs
- a milk jug
- cake stands/china, crystal or silver platters/pretty vintage floral serving plates

Plan your menu; it should be possible to eat everything in small bites – if so, the only extra cutlery should be the knife to spread the jam. If others are bringing large cakes then provide cake stands and cake slices and remember to provide dainty forks to eat the cakes with.

Table decorations

A large, low-level flower arrangement, little vases of wild flowers, or big soft-pink roses will add a pretty finishing touch to your table. Don't put water in the vases, as at some point your guests will knock the flowers over and the water will soak the tablecloth. Loose petals are another pretty touch, as is edible gold leaf, which you can sprinkle on top of the tea.

In the style of true Victorian excess, I like to add unusual ornaments to the table. You can also add scattered jewellery and old fashioned photos in frames.

How to dress

It is always important to look your best. As Elizabeth Hurley once said, "why look bad when you can look good?!" A classic Victorian-style tea party is an opportunity to wear your best frock and new shoes. There will be no dancing, so rest assured you can wear heels and look rather stylish. This is also a fabulous time to get out your vintage pieces – you can wear hats, gloves, necklaces and brooches and make a real event of it. For those who want to dedicate themselves to true Victorian style, enormous, feathered and flower-laden hats were very fashionable and uncorseted tea gowns were worn for informal entertaining at home during this era. Keep hair tied back in feminine pleats and twists. Accessorise with parasols and fans and pretty purses.

Entertainment

Play music that is conducive to the situation and keep it at an appropriate level, don't play it so loud that it will compete with the conversation. If you notice people leaning in to hear each other, the music is too loud. Play classical music in the background throughout the tea, but, if you wish, hire a pianist for true ambience.

Tea and how to serve it

Tea was once so expensive and precious that it would be locked up in a tea caddy by the hostess. English aristocrats would serve variations of black tea and created a ceremony that is pretty similar to the one we have adopted today. There are many different teas, which I will mention later in this chapter along with the classic method for preparing and serving tea (see pages 42–45).

The only argument is do you put the milk in first or last?

Here are some historical opinions:
The original and very delicate teacups would shatter if the hot tea was poured in first, hence milk first... People only started putting milk in last when china cups were used – as a status symbol to show off that you could afford better than a clay mug... The footman would prepare the tea in the pot on a tray, then pour the tea from the pot into the china cups which he would hand round. He would then pass round a tray with the milk jug and sugar lumps with little tongs, so you could add milk and sugar to your taste.

There is no right or wrong to this dilemma! Betty Blythe believes it should be as *you* wish.

THE VICTORIAN TEA PARTY CHECKLIST

- A setting of elegance and sophistication
- Tables and chairs
- Tablecloth
- Napkins
- Crockery
- Cake stands
- Cake knives
- Tea (loose or bags)
- Tea strainer
- Milk and milk jug
- Perfectly pouring tea pot
- White sugar lumps, sugar bowl and tongs
- Savoury food
- Cakes and scones
- Cream and jam
- Elegant attire
- Pretty accessories
- Victorian-style outfits (optional)
- Don't forget your etiquette

Betty Blythe's guide to tea party etiquette

Greet everyone with a handshake and a polite "how do you do?"

Keep purses on laps or behind you on your chair – never on the table.

Remain seated and wait for things to be done for you by the hostess (unless you arrange someone to do the serving for you).

Napkins should be placed on your lap. If you must leave the table temporarily, leave it on the chair.

Never reach across the table for anything. Instead, ask to be passed something – there's no hurry.

For "full tea" three courses are served, such as tea sandwiches, scones and sweets. A "light tea" has just scones and sweets.

If all the courses are laid out on the table, eat them in this order: first the tiny sandwiches, scones or muffins, and last the sweeter treats. Think of it as a meal where you start with bread, then have the main course, but save the sweetest part for last.

You can eat with your fingers. However, if an item is particularly messy (has a runny or crumbly filling, for instance), then use a fork.

For scones or muffins, break off a bite-size piece, then put a small amount of jam or butter on it. If Devonshire or clotted cream is available, a small amount can be dabbed on after the jam. This thick cream is for the scones, not for the tea.

Take bites of the tiny sandwiches. Never put the whole thing in your mouth, even though it's small.

If taking sugar in your tea, be careful to not dip the sugar tong or sugar spoon into the tea.

Stir sugar and/or milk with the teaspoon, then place the teaspoon on the saucer behind the cup.

When drinking tea, Victorians would hold the cup and saucer near to their chests, then bring the teacup up to their mouths to drink.

If the tea is hot, leave the teacup on the table to cool. Do not blow on the tea.

Hold the teacup normally. Do not slurp. Do not stick your pinkie out when drinking tea – it's really not necessary.

Finally, always send a handwritten note of thanks to the host.

Victoria Sponge
with Fresh Strawberries and Cream

Enjoyed by royalty so much that it took Queen Victoria's name, this glorious sponge cake is universally loved. Perfect for afternoon gatherings – it shouldn't be seen without a lovingly prepared pot of tea.

Serves 6–8

225 g/8 oz/1 cup unsalted butter, softened, plus extra for greasing

225 g/8 oz/1⅛ cups caster (superfine) sugar

4 large eggs, lightly beaten ✳ finely grated zest and juice of 1 lemon

225 g/8 oz/scant 1⅔ cups self-raising (self-rising) flour, sifted, plus extra for dusting

FOR THE FILLING

150 g/5 oz good-quality strawberry jam ✳ 250 g/9 oz/1¾ cups fresh strawberries, hulled and sliced

1 vanilla pod (bean) ✳ 300 ml/10 fl oz/1¼ cups double (heavy) cream

1½ tbsp caster (superfine) sugar ✳ icing (confectioners') sugar, for dusting

Preheat the oven to 180°C/350°F/Gas Mark 4. Grease and line 2 x 17 cm/6½ in loose-based cake tins, then grease again with butter and coat with 2 tbsp of the sugar to crisp the edges of the cake.

Using an electric mixer, beat the remaining sugar and the butter together until pale and light. Beat in the eggs a little at a time to make a mousse-like consistency, then finely grate in the zest of the lemon (reserving the juice of the lemon for the filling). Fold in the flour using a wooden spoon and divide the cake mixture between the prepared tins, spreading out the mixture gently. Bake for about 25 minutes until well risen and golden brown and an inserted skewer comes out clean. Leave to cool in the tin for 10 minutes before turning out onto a rack to cool.

To make the filling, warm the jam in a pan over a low heat, then remove from the heat and stir in the sliced strawberries. Carefully score the vanilla pod lengthways and scrape out all the seeds. Pour the cream into a bowl, add the caster sugar and vanilla seeds, then squeeze in the reserved lemon juice. Whip until you have nice soft peaks. Spread the jam and strawberries mixture evenly over one layer of the cake, then spread the sweetened cream over the top of the strawberries. Place the second half of the cake on top, with the pretty side facing up, and dust with icing sugar before serving.

Mini Mixed Fruit Tartlets

Little bites of deliciousness, these dainty tartlet cases can be made a day in advance and kept in an airtight container. To decorate, I use raspberries, grapes, kiwi and lavender-frosted blueberries, but pretty much any fruit will do.

Makes 15–20 tartlets

115 g/4 oz/generous ¾ cup plain (all-purpose) flour, plus extra for dusting
55 g/2 oz/¼ cup chilled unsalted butter, diced ● 30 g/1 oz/¼ cup icing (confectioners') sugar, sifted
finely grated zest of 1 orange ● 1 egg yolk ● 1 tbsp cold orange juice

For the filling

200 g/7 oz/1⅓ cups blueberries ● 1 egg white, beaten ● 100 g/3½ oz/½ cup lavender sugar
250 g/9 oz shop-bought custard ● 100 g/3½ oz/generous ¾ cup raspberries
2 kiwi fruits, cut in half and sliced ● 20 g/¾ oz green grapes, sliced in half
satsuma or orange zest swirls, to decorate

First, make the lavender-frosted blueberries. In a large bowl, coat the blueberries with the egg white. Place the lavender sugar on a large tray and coat the blueberries in the sugar. Leave to dry at room temperature.

Next, make the pastry. Sift the flour into a mixing bowl, add the butter and, using your fingertips, rub it in until the mixture resembles fine breadcrumbs. Stir in the sugar and orange zest. Lightly beat the egg yolk with the cold orange juice, then add it to the flour mixture and mix in with a knife. Gather together to make a soft dough. Don't over-handle the mixture. Wrap the dough in cling film and chill in the refrigerator for at least 30 minutes.

Roll the dough out on a lightly floured surface and line your tartlet tins with it. Prick the bases with a fork and chill for 20 minutes.

Meanwhile, preheat the oven to 200°C/400°F/Gas Mark 6. Line the tartlet tins with baking parchment and fill with baking beans, then blind bake for 10–15 minutes, until the edges are golden. Remove the beans and baking parchment and cook for a further 5 minutes. Leave to cool.

Once the tartlet cases have cooled, fill each with 1 tbsp of the custard, then top with the fruit and the lavender-frosted blueberries. Decorate with satsuma zest swirls to finish.

Delightful Finger Sandwiches

Ah! The Sandwich – defining the English afternoon tea. Tea sandwiches know their place – that is, before the scones and well before the cake.

SERVES 6–8
1 white farmhouse loaf
50 g/1¾ oz/4 tbsp salted butter, at room temperature ● 1 rye farmhouse loaf

FOR THE COOL CUCUMBER SANDWICHES
½ medium cucumber, thinly sliced
2 tbsp white wine vinegar ● salt and freshly ground black pepper

FOR THE SMOKED SALMON, DILL AND CREAM CHEESE SANDWICHES
juice of 1 lemon ● 4 tbsp cream cheese ● 4 fresh dill sprigs
70 g/2½ oz smoked salmon slices

FOR THE ROAST BEEF AND WATERCRESS SANDWICHES
1 tbsp wholegrain mustard ● 70 g/2½ oz roast beef, thinly sliced
1 handful of watercress

For the Cool Cucumber sandwiches, place the cucumber and vinegar in a bowl and season with salt and pepper. Leave to stand for 30 minutes while preparing the other sandwiches. Once the cucumber is ready, butter 4 slices of white bread on each side. Layer the cucumbers slices on the butter and place the second buttered slice of bread on top. Cut off the crusty edges and carefully slice into 4 fingers.

For the Smoked Salmon, Dill and Cream Cheese sandwiches, mix the lemon juice and cream cheese together in a bowl until it is a smooth consistency. Spread the cream cheese on 4 slices of white bread. Top 2 of the slices with a few sprigs of dill and salmon slices. Sandwich with the remaining prepared slices. Cut off the crusts and carefully slice into 4 fingers.

For the Roast Beef and Watercress sandwiches, butter 4 slices of the rye bread. Spread the mustard over 2 slices of the buttered bread, then layer the roast beef over the mustard. Finish off the sandwich by removing any large stalks from the watercress and placing on top of the roast beef. Sandwich with the remaining buttered slices. Cut off the crusts and carefully slice into 4 fingers.

Mini Cherry Scones
with Raspberry and Rose Jam

These simple scones are the jewel in the crown of this occasion. Sweet little cherries sparkle throughout and the whole is graced by rose-kissed raspberry jam.

Mini Cherry Scones

SERVES 6–8

450 g/1 lb/3¼ cups self-raising (self-rising) flour, plus extra for dusting

¼ tsp salt ✳ 1 tsp bicarbonate of soda (baking soda)

100 g/3½oz/7 tbsp cold butter, diced

2 tbsp caster (superfine) sugar

280 ml/10 fl oz/1¼ cups buttermilk

2 tbsp milk ✳ 2 tsp vanilla extract

90 g/3 oz dried cherries, roughly chopped

227 g/8 oz tub of Devonshire clotted cream, to serve

Preheat the oven to 200°C/400°F/Gas Mark 6.

Put the flour, salt, bicarbonate of soda and butter into a bowl and,
using your fingertips, rub in the butter until the mixture resembles breadcrumbs.
Mix in the sugar, then quickly mix in the buttermilk, a splash of milk,
the vanilla extract and cherries and bring together to form a soft dough.
Try not to knead, as the dough will become tough.

Press the dough out onto a lightly floured surface to about 2 cm/¾ in thickness and,
using 4 cm/1½ in cutters, cut out 15–17 rounds. Transfer the rounds to a lightly floured baking
sheet, brush with the remaining milk and bake for 12–15 minutes until golden and well risen.
Serve with Devonshire clotted cream and the Raspberry and Rose Jam (see following recipe).

Continues...

Raspberry and Rose Jam

MAKES 3 X 200 ML/7 FL OZ JARS
450 g/1 lb/3¾ cups raspberries, rinsed
500 g/1 lb 2 oz/2½ cups granulated sugar
juice of 1 lemon ❁ 3 tbsp rose essence

Place 2 saucers in the freezer. This is to test the setting and consistency of the jam.

Place the raspberries in a pan and cook over a gentle heat for 2–3 minutes until the juices are just beginning to run. Add the sugar and lemon juice and stir over a gentle heat for 1–2 minutes until the sugar has dissolved. Increase the heat and bring to a vigorous boil for 10–15 minutes. Turn the heat down, add the rose essence and leave to simmer for 10 minutes.

Remove the pan from the heat and test the jam by dabbing a little onto one of the cooled saucers. Leave to cool for a few seconds, then push the jam with your fingertip. If it wrinkles, the jam is set and ready. If not, boil for a further 5 minutes then test again. When the setting point is reached carefully spoon the jam into sterilized jam jars and leave to cool. When cool, pop on the lids.

The jam will keep for up to 3 weeks.

Chocolate Marble Cake

Some of the earliest references to cakes are found in ancient Roman history, so they have been around for a long while. This one certainly won't last long, as your guests cut through the ganache icing and marvel at the marble within.

SERVES 6–8
125 g/4½ oz/½ cup unsalted butter, plus some for greasing
100 g/3½ oz/½ cup caster (superfine) sugar ❀ 2 medium eggs
1 tsp vanilla extract ❀ 250 g/9 oz/1¾ cups plain (all-purpose) flour
2 tsp baking powder ❀ pinch of salt
125 ml/4 fl oz/½ cup milk, plus 1 tbsp ❀ 1 tbsp (unsweetened) cocoa powder

FOR THE CHOCOLATE GANACHE
25 g/1 oz/2 tbsp unsalted butter ❀ 2 tbsp double (heavy) cream
60 g/2½ oz dark (semisweet) chocolate, finely chopped
125 g/4½ oz/generous 1 cup icing (confectioners') sugar, sifted
½ tsp vanilla extract

Preheat the oven to 180°C/350°F/Gas Mark 4. Grease a 22 cm/8½ in fluted ring bundt pan with butter.

Using an electric mixer, beat the butter and sugar together until pale and creamy. Slowly beat in the eggs and vanilla extract, then fold in the flour, baking powder, salt and milk. Once the mixture is evenly combined, divide it in two, put each half into 2 separate bowls and add the cocoa powder and 1 tbsp of milk to one half. Spoon a thin layer of the white cake mixture into the prepared pan followed by a layer of the chocolate mixture, and repeat twice. Trace the number 8 through the cake mixture to marble, making sure the knife is touching the base of the pan.

Bake for 40–45 minutes. Leave for 15 minutes before transferring to a wire rack to cool.

To make the ganache, melt the butter and cream in a small saucepan, making sure that the mixture doesn't boil. Remove from the heat and stir in the chocolate, vanilla and sugar. Once all the ingredients are combined and the chocolate has melted pour over the cake. Leave to cool and serve with a lovely cup of tea.

Making Tea

Every home should have a selection of teas, and it is certainly a well kept home
that can offer surprise guests a tea of their preference rather than an average teabag.
Tea can be refreshing, calming and, as its drinkers gossip away, an unknowing accompaniment
to scandal and misfortune.

Tea is made from the leaves of the *Camellia sinensis* plant, which is native to the Far East.
The tea leaf is dried, oxidized or fermented, baked, fried or roasted to produce the better known
black teas, green teas and white teas. Tea can be purchased loose and in pre-made bags.
If you visit a fine tea merchant they can advise you on the nature of each tea available.
They also have a larger selection of teas to choose from and you can buy teas to
try in smaller quantities here.

The first teabags were made from silk and muslin (cheesecloth), but today teabags are
mostly made from paper, which is produced from a blend of wool and vegetable (hemp) fibres.
Both wood and vegetable pulp are usually chlorine bleached meaning that a small amount of chlorine
compounds may end up in the teabag paper, which can certainly make the tea taste unpleasant.

Proper storage of tea is essential as, if kept improperly, it will lose its subtle flavour.
Tea should always be stored at a constant temperature in an airtight container away from light,
moisture and strong odours, and not in the refrigerator.

Tea contains caffeine, a natural element in the leaves – the blacker the tea the higher the level.
To avoid caffeine try drinking white and green teas as these are lower in caffeine.
Alternatively, try herbal tisanes as a wonderful way of taking part in the tea drinking experience.

The delicate art of brewing tea with loose leaves will add a civilized and genteel touch
to your afternoon tea party. As you slow down the pace with this calm and elegant ancient ritual you
leave plenty of time for good conversation, and your guests will certainly appreciate the time taken
to prepare their beverage.

Classic types of tea

ASSAM
The preferred tea of the British, this is
a bold full-bodied malty tea, which is best
drunk with milk; it is wonderful to start
the day with.

DARJEELING
Known as the champagne of teas, lightly
coloured and fruity, this delicate
and highly aromatic tea is perfect
for the afternoon.

CEYLON
Bright and golden with an intense crisp
and refreshing flavour, this is a tea
to enjoy at any time of the day.

LAPSANG SOUCHONG
With its golden colour, the distinctive
wood-smoked taste of this tea is best
drunk black (or with just a very little milk,
though ill advised!).

JASMINE
To be enjoyed without milk, this tea
is scented with jasmine flowers and has
a sweet delicate aroma.

EARL GREY
The fragrant blend of black tea and
bergamot creates a smoky and citrusy
flavour. It is best served black with a slice
of lemon and goes exquisitely with cakes
and sweet delights.

What do I need to make a perfect pot of tea?

Tea ❋ Water ❋ Kettle
Teapot (porcelain or oriental cast-iron style)
Strainer ❋ Teacup and saucer

Once you're sure you have everything ready, start by filling your kettle with the amount of cold water you need, and be sure to remember to add a little extra, as the tea will soak the water up. When you have the correct amount, switch the kettle on to boil.

While the water is heating up, it's time to preheat the teapot and the teacups. To do this, use hot tap water to fill them. It is always important to preheat the teapot and tea cups – if they are cold when you add the boiling water to make the tea, some of the heat will be lost, making the tea cooler than desired. Leave the hot tap water in until they are sufficiently warmed.

Shortly before the kettle comes to a boil, empty water out of the teapot and add your tea leaves.

Use approximately 1 heaped teaspoon per 225 ml/8 fl oz/1 cup water. If you like your tea a little stronger, then add as much as you need for your required taste. If you are using bags, add one for each person and an extra one for the pot, as the saying goes.

Add the boiled water to the teapot. Remember not to fill it too high, as you can sometimes lose water from the lid when pouring tea in front of your seated guests. Proceed to steep it for the appropriate amount of time: For green tea, steep for 2–3 minutes, for black teas, 3–5 minutes, and for herbal teas, 5 minutes or more. Pay attention that you do not steep for any longer than this, as it will not make the tea stronger, just more bitter. So remember if you want a stronger cup of tea, simply add more tea leaves!

Your guests are waiting patiently as you prepare the teacups, sugar bowl, milk jug and lemon slices on the tray. Lay it down on a stable surface and pour the tea carefully into the cups. Relax and enjoy.

Edwardian Breakfast

At country house parties in the early years of this century, breakfast was a veritable feast. High society Edwardians enjoyed living in a whirlwind of social engagements, and their days started and finished with luxury goods such as melons, goose and fine wines. Breakfast was a time to fill up on delicious morsels and it makes a great "tea party" occasion in itself. It is a wonderful opportunity to gather friends together, perhaps as an after-party to the previous night's event, or as a hearty start to a weekend's activities. Step back in time and enjoy the breakfast dishes of a more leisurely era.

❋ Menu ❋

Orange and Apple Marmalade,
served with Muffins

Porridge with Honeycomb

Herbed Kedgeree

Mixed Grill

Chocolate Bundle Pastries

Juices

Coffee

Breakfast cocktails:
Ruby Breakfast Cocktail
& Arabica Espresso Martini

Setting the scene

Edwardian aristocrats and those who aspired to the high living of this time divided their breakfast into two: formal or informal. You can choose which style you want to emulate:

Formal breakfast: held at any time between 10am and 12:30. A fruit course opened the menu: melons cut in slices, baskets of apples, pears and peaches, with grapes hanging heavily over the rim. This was followed by both a mild *hors d'oeuvre* such as devilled eggs, and then the main breakfast plates were laid. A pot of hot chocolate was served with a cooked breakfast: this would consist of beef steak or lamb chops, with a salad of sliced tomatoes or lettuce, hard-boiled eggs, or poached eggs on toast; or omelette with muffins and butter. Smoked haddock was the favourite breakfast fish and sometimes lobster was served. For the next course: chicken, broiled or fried with rice. A dessert of frozen punch, pastry or jellies followed; and, finally, coffee, in breakfast cups like oversized tea cups, concluded the meal.

Informal breakfast: less elaborate and would have been served at 10 or 11am. It began with fruit, and may be followed by ham or bacon and eggs with a fried potato dish. Alternatively, porridge served with cream would be followed by broiled haddock and baked potatoes. For a hint of sweetness, breakfast buns with marmalade or honey would conclude this breakfast.

If you don't already own a large Edwardian house to accommodate your guests then do not fear! Many wonderful houses are available to rent for a weekend – pack your cases and arrive in style. Alternatively, furnish your dining room with a round dark wood table and side furniture.

Announcing the breakfast

Where great formality is observed, it is customary to knock at the bedroom door of the guests, to announce breakfast. Otherwise, a gong or bell may be used to summon the guests to the table.

Presentation

Ideally, breakfast would be served on the polished tabletop, and in the English fashion. It will be necessary to place several tablemats under hot platters, to preserve the table from heat stains. Alternatively, one could decide to use a heavy cover of felt or similar material to protect the tabletop, and spread over this a snowy white damask tablecloth (monogrammed, if possible). Sometimes over this could be placed still another cloth of elaborate embroidery and lace.

At the centre of the table, place a dish of fruit, a growing plant, or cut flowers, and at each end a handsome candelabra. Compotiers or little dishes which stand on either side of the centrepiece, can be filled with favours for the ladies, and may be anything that the fancy dictates.

The plates, of breakfast size, usually white with gold or silver rims, and cutlery are set half an inch from the edge of the table. White napkins, glasses, and muffin plates are set in place for each individual at the beginning of the meal.

At the right of the plate, lay a knife, the cutting edge turned towards the plate. At the right of the knife, lay a dessert spoon for the porridge. On the left of the plate, lay a fork of breakfast size, with tines turned upward. At the point of the knife, set a tumbler of water, then glasses for whatever other beverages are intended to be served. At the point of

the fork, set a small plate for bread, hot muffins, and butter, and across this lay a small knife. At the left of the fork, lay a napkin, above the plate, set a dessert spoon, and above this a fruit napkin with a finger-bowl beside it. Between each two covers, set out salt and pepper sets, and carafes for water. For an attractive touch, use pretty cut-glass decanters.

Above the cover at the foot of the table, set out the required number of coffee cups and saucers – a large tray often holds the whole coffee service. Near these, lay the coffee spoons on a flat dish, the cream-jug, and a bowl of cut sugar.

Music

Edwardians would play their records on phonograph cylinders, but live performances, both amateur and professional, were popular. Listen to classical pieces from Henry Wood, Edward Elgar, Gustav Holst, Arnold Bax, and George Butterworth.

Orange and Apple Marmalade

Keep the doctor away by starting your day with this apple and orange marmalade. This sweet version is divine smothered over muffins – you will wonder why breakfast should not be like this every day.

MAKES 4 X 450 G/1 LB JAM JARS
6 large orange or four small ones ● 3 Cox apples, cored, peeled and roughly chopped
1 kg/2 lb 4 oz/5 cups jam sugar (sugar with pectin)
500 g/1 lb 2 oz/2½ cups white caster (superfine) sugar
4 tbsp lemon juice ● 3 tbsp water

Using a vegetable peeler, remove the zest from the oranges, making sure that there is no pith left on the zest. Slice the zest thinly and set aside. Peel the white pith away from the oranges, then squeeze the juice into a large heavy-based saucepan. Chop the flesh from the oranges finely.

Place the remaining ingredients into the saucepan together with the oranges and bring the mixture to the boil over a high heat. Reduce the heat and leave to simmer for 35 minutes, skimming off any foam with a slotted spoon.

Sterilize 4 jam jars by pouring boiling water onto the lids and jars. Ladle the marmalade into the jars, leaving a 2 cm/¾ in gap from the top. Place the lids on the jars, then turn the jars upside down for 5 minutes to seal the lids. Turn the jars upright and leave to cool. If you have time, leave the jam to stand for a day or two, as the taste of the marmalade becomes better with time. Serve with a warm, buttered muffin.

Porridge with Honeycomb

Celebrate this golden era with this delicious version of porridge, spiced with cinnamon and laced with honeycomb, for a delightful start to the morning.

SERVES 6–8
300 g/9 oz/3 cups traditional rolled oats * 900 ml/1½ pints/3½ cups full cream milk
360 ml/12½ fl oz/generous 1½ cups boiling water
1½ tsp ground cinnamon * large pinch of salt * 250 g/9 oz honeycomb

Combine the oats, milk, boiling water, cinnamon and salt in a saucepan, place over a high heat and bring to the boil. Reduce the heat to low and cook, stirring with a wooden spoon, for 5 minutes, or until the porridge thickens and covers the spoon.

Remove from the heat, then cover and leave to stand for 10 minutes (the porridge will cool and thicken slightly on standing). Spoon the porridge into bowls and finish with a tablespoon of honeycomb to serve.

Chocolate Bundle Pastries

The Edwardians loved to drink hot chocolate for breakfast, so I have incorporated chocolate into these decadent pastries. They certainly did not watch their waistlines and now is not a time to think of yours either! Indulge in these chocolatey nutty bundles to make breakfast-time a treat.

SERVES 8

375 g/13 oz ready-rolled puff pastry
50 g/1¾ oz good-quality dark (semisweet) chocolate (at least 70% cocoa solids), roughly chopped
50 g/1¾ oz good-quality milk chocolate, roughly chopped
50 g/1¾ oz good-quality white chocolate, roughly chopped
70 g/2½ oz/scant ¾ cup walnuts, toasted and roughly chopped
1 medium egg, lightly beaten

Preheat the oven to 200°C/400°F/Gas Mark 6.

Cut the pastry into 8 equal squares. Place ½ tbsp of each type of chocolate and ½ tsp of the walnuts into the middle of each square. Bring each corner to the middle and twist, making sure to secure all 4 corners together. Using a pastry brush, brush with the beaten egg and bake in the oven for 12–15 minutes, or until golden brown. Serve warm.

Herbed Kedgeree

Kedgeree can be traced back to the year 1340. It is widely believed that the dish was brought to the UK by returning British colonials who had enjoyed it in India and brought it back to Victorian Britain. This rice dish containing smoked haddock and boiled egg was an Edwardian staple and a delicious breakfast dish. I think that the coriander makes this dish that extra bit special and I would eat this every day if I could!

Serves 6–8

FOR THE CRISPY ONIONS
3 tbsp sunflower oil knob of butter
2 large white onions, peeled, halved and thinly sliced

FOR THE RICE
2 tbsp vegetable oil ● 2 large onions, peeled and finely chopped
2 tsp coriander seeds, crushed ● 1 tsp cumin seeds, crushed
2 tsp ground turmeric ● 2 cardamon pods, bruised
3 tsp Madras curry powder ● salt ● 400 g/14 oz/2 cups basmati rice, rinsed
100 g/3½ oz/generous ½ cup mixed sultanas (golden raisins) and raisins
1 cinnamon stick ● 700 ml/1¼ pints/3 cups water ● 12 quail's eggs
600 g/1 lb 5 oz undyed smoked haddock fillet, skin on ● 2 bay leaves
500 ml/17 fl oz/generous 2 cups milk ● juice of 2 lemons
2 red chillies, deseeded and chopped
good handful of chopped parsley, plus extra for sprinkling (optional)
good handful of chopped coriander, plus extra for sprinkling (optional)

For the crispy onions, place a large frying pan over a high heat and add the oil and butter.
Add the onions and cook until soft, making sure not to colour the onions.
Reduce the heat to low and keep stirring until golden brown, about 15 minutes.
Transfer the onions to a plate lined with kitchen paper and set aside.

Continues...

For the rice, heat the oil in a large lidded pan.
Add the chopped onions and gently fry for 5 minutes until softened, but not coloured.
Add the coriander, cumin, turmeric, cardamom pods and curry powder,
then season generously with salt and continue to fry until the mixture starts
to go brown and fragrant, about 3 minutes.

Add the rice, the mixed sultanas and raisins, the cinnamon stick and water,
then stir and bring to the boil. Reduce the heat to a simmer, cover with a tight fitting lid and
cook for 10 minutes Remove from the heat and leave to stand, covered, for a further 10–15 minutes.
The rice will be perfectly cooked if you do not lift the lid before the end of the cooking.

While the rice is cooking place the quail's eggs in a small saucepan of cold water.
Bring to the boil, then reduce the heat and count to 20 seconds. They should now be hard-boiled.
Remove from the heat and rinse under cold running water. Peel immediately.

Put the haddock and bay leaves in a frying pan, cover with the milk and poach for 10 minutes
until the flesh flakes easily. Remove the fish from the milk, peel away the skin,
then flake the flesh into medium pieces.

Once the rice has cooked, break it up with a fork and gently pour over the lemon juice.
Mix in the chillies, fish, eggs, chopped parsley and coriander. Serve hot,
sprinkled with a few extra herbs and your crispy onions.

Mixed Grill

A hearty appetite is needed to do justice to this magnificent breakfast feast.

SERVES 6–8

800 g/1 lb 12 oz Maris Piper potatoes, peeled

6 spring onions (scallions), trimmed and thinly sliced

1 large egg ❋ salt and freshly ground black pepper

4 tbsp sunflower (canola) oil

FOR THE SAUSAGES

8 smoked streaky (lean) bacon rashers (slices)

8 pork sausages ❋ 2 tbsp olive oil

FOR THE MIXED MUSHROOMS AND GRILLED VINE TOMATOES

4 vines of Midi plum tomatoes, kept on the vine ❋ 3 tbsp olive oil

3 garlic cloves, peeled and minced ❋ 1 large knob (piece) of butter

250 g/9 oz portobello mushrooms, sliced into quarters

125 g/4½ oz oyster mushrooms, sliced in half

250 g/9 oz/3½ cups chestnut (cremini) mushrooms, thinly sliced

1 lemon ❋ pinch of cayenne peppe

handful of flat-leaf parsley, roughly chopped

FOR THE BLACK PUDDING

2 tbsp sunflower (canola) oil

400 g/14 oz black pudding (blood sausage)

Preheat oven to 180°C/350°F/Gas Mark 4.

First, make the rösti. Finely grate the potatoes, then place in kitchen paper and wring out until there is no more liquid from the potato. Put the grated potato in a bowl with the spring onions and salt and pepper and mix together.

Continues...

Heat 2 tbsp sunflower oil in a large frying pan over a medium heat.
Using a dessertspoon, place 4 rounded heaps of the potato mixture in the oil and slightly flatten
with the back of the spoon. Fry, turning the potato mix constantly, until golden.
Remove from the pan and leave to drain on a plate lined with kitchen paper.
Continue until the mixture is finished. Place the röstis on a foil-lined baking tray and set aside.

For the sausages, line a medium baking tray with foil.
Wrap the streaky bacon around the sausages, making sure to tuck the end of the bacon into one of
the folds so they don't unwrap. Coat with the olive oil and cook in the oven on the central shelf
for 20–25 minutes, turning halfway to brown evenly.

For the mushrooms and tomatoes, line another baking tray with foil. Place the tomatoes on the lined tray
and drizzle with 2 tbsp of the olive oil. Season well, place in the oven on the top shelf and bake
for 15–20 minutes. Place the tray with the rösti on in the oven on the bottom shelf.

To cook the mushrooms, heat the remaining 1 tbsp olive oil in a medium-sized frying pan.
Add the garlic and fry for 30 seconds, then add the butter followed by the mushrooms and fry for 6 minutes
until cooked and coated in the garlic oil mixture. Squeeze the lemon over the mushrooms, add the cayenne
and season well. Remove the mushrooms with a slotted spoon and set aside.

Finally, cook the black pudding. Heat the sunflower oil in a medium-sized pan.
Add the black pudding and fry for 2 minutes, then flip over and continue to cook for 1 more minute.

Remove the sausages, rösti and tomatoes from the oven and serve with the black pudding,
mushrooms, a strong coffee and some warm, buttered bread.

Ruby Breakfast Cocktail

Never mind the breakfast juice, liven up your day with this morning cocktail!

SERVES 1

12.5 ml/2½ tsp sloe gin ✻ 12.5 ml/2½ tsp Chambord (raspberry liqueur)
12.5 ml/2½ tsp Absolut Citron vodka ✻ 12.5 ml/2½ tsp Cointreau ✻ 12.5 ml/2½ tsp lime juice
12.5ml/2½ tsp lemon juice ✻ 100 ml/3½ fl oz/scant ½ cup blood orange juice ✻ grenadine

Add all the ingredients into a cocktail shaker. Shake and strain all ingredients into your chosen glass.
For a more pristine finish, fine strain to remove pulp.

This can be served in any manner one desires, as a fruity martini or tall on the rocks for longer-lasting
refreshment, but it is certainly a welcome accompaniment for an Edwardian breakfast feast.

Arabica Espresso Martini

Add an extra kick to your morning coffee in true Edwardian style.

SERVES 1

3 green cardamom pods, plus extra cardamom pods to garnish
1 espresso shot ✻ 25 ml/1 fl oz/2 tbsp vodka ✻ 25 ml/1 fl oz/2 tbsp kahlua

Grind three cardamom pods in a pestle and mortar and place into the bottom of a glass. Decant the espresso
into the glass and leave for a minute to infuse. Pour into a cocktail shaker full of ice and add the rest of the
ingredients. Shake and fine strain into a glass and garnish delicately with some more cardamom pods,
which should rest easily on the froth.

1920's Speakeasy

It's the Roaring Twenties – the era of Prohibition. Bars are closed due to heavy saloon license fees and underground establishments that illegally sell alcoholic beverages have sprung up in their place. The young wild folks, known as "flappers and dappers", drink, smoke and dance all night at these "speakeasies", having a good time and getting a little "loosey-goosey" without having to worry about being in trouble for doing so.

This is a fun theme for birthday parties or inventive engagement parties. Whether you choose to hire a venue with a bar already set up, or use your own joint, get ready for a wild evening of jazz, canapés, Champagne and Manhattans. Why, you'll be the cat's pyjamas!

Menu

Bresaola and Parmesan Crostini

Waldorf Salad Crostini

Harissa Chicken Skewers with
Sumac Yogurt Dip

Halloumi Skewers with Parsley Oil

Chocolate and Hazelnut Strawberries

Cocktails: Queen of Sheba,
Minty Fresh, Surrendering Sloe,
& Los Angeles Sunset

Setting the scene

While the vast majority of speakeasies were dank, dingy places serving near-inedible food and bathtub liquors, a few existed that truly were the kind of swanky joints we see in the movies. These select speakeasies were glamorous, high-class establishments that offered food and entertainment. Some of them were operated by people who were part of organized crime. Pick up this theme and encourage your guests to dress as gangsters and their molls. Even though police and agents of the Bureau of Prohibition would often raid speakeasy parties and arrest their owners and patrons, they were so profitable that they continued to flourish.

Location

The entrance to the party should be very humble to the point of being hard to find. The speakeasies of New York legend were hidden behind toy stores, or entered through fake phone booths. Guests should have to search hard to find the party – the less glamorous, the better. There should be no obvious sign that there are hinky things goings on. If you have a back door or side entrance use it. To identify your joint, use a building number or a green flag or one broken bulb. This one detail will need to be included in the invitation. You could have a bouncer on the door. An absolute must is a special knock, a password from popular 1920's slang, or an object to be handed in at the door (a popular item was a library book – if a raid occurred they claimed to be reading clubs). Again, this must be mentioned on the invitation.

Decor

To create the intimate, secretive vibe of a speakeasy, decorate your room with dark, rich fabrics, faux furs and velvet, for a lavish touch. Provide small, round tables with chairs and cover the tables in heavy tablecloths. The lighting should be subdued – pop a few low-level lamps or small candle holders on the tables – empty liquor bottles fashioned into candelabras are another fun touch.

Bartenders should be in some sort of uniform. Provide drinks in crystal glasses or use innocent little teacups and saucers for your cocktails – this was the traditional way to serve alcohol at a speakeasy back in the Roaring Twenties. Serve your canapés from silver platters and glass plates, with shiny red or black tableware.

Create a background with props, including violin cases (notoriously used to hide Tommy guns), dusty antique books, art deco paintings, flapper prints or vintage-style alcohol adverts, photographs of Al Capone, Bonnie and Clyde, or any other famous gangster of that time period. Print out tabloid newspapers and leave them around the place. Promote the retro bar ambience by purchasing old-looking bottles from secondhand stores and online.

If you are having the party at your house or somewhere that has a bath, fill the tub with water and ice to keep your drinks cold – you can call it "bathtub gin".

Use your television to play old silent films in the background. Play music, but hide your modern system with antique linen or a tablecloth.

Music

The 1920s saw the height of New Orleans and Chicago styles of jazz, sandwiched between the Dixieland sound of the 1900s and the Swing era of the 1930s. Fill your play list with authentic 1920's sounds: pianist and bandleader Jelly Roll Morton, Louis Armstrong and his Hot Five, cornetist Bix Beiderbecke, pianist Earl Hines, pianist James P. Johnson, and saxophonist-clarinetist Sidney Bechet.

If you have the budget, the sound of a live upbeat jazz band will add a wonderful energy to your evening! A pianist, with a singing Sheba, is also rather swanky.

Invitations

Send out Art Deco-style black and white invitations. These days you have the choice of sending online or mailed invitations, but using the old-fashioned postal way will add to the intrigue. Whichever way you choose, make sure that you grab your guest's attention and be sure to mention what attire you would like them to wear.

"...Come drink & dance the night away at our Roaring '20s Speakeasy Party...."

"...The booze will be flowing like milk and honey, Honey!...."

"...Dress as a gangster or silent screen star; Come as a flapper or come as you are...."

What to wear

Ladies

In the 1920s, a new woman was born: she smoked, drank, danced, and voted; she cut her hair, wore heavy make-up; she was giddy and took risks. She was a Flapper. The typical flapper look comprised a short, finger-waved bob with a feathered headband, a drop-waisted, fringed or heavily beaded cocktail dress, over-the-knee stockings and a sexy pair of round-toed heels. Accessorise this look with a long cigarette holder, a long string of pearls, and a feather boa. Flappers often finished the ensemble with a felt, bell-shaped hat called a cloche. Also, as a speakeasy was the only place to get a decent drink, so no respectable flapper would be seen without her personal hipflask neatly tied to her leg.

Chaps

Some speakeasies were used as homes and offices by gangsters, who adopted an extravagant lifestyle. Successful gangsters could be identified by their fashionable silk suits, expensive jewellery, and guns. Men – you can't put on any old rags. Emulate the style of Al Capone – think pin-striped suits with fedora hats. Black or white ties on a black shirt, spats (white canvas or vinyl shoe covers). Don't be a "gooseberry lay" – check out the internet's supply of men's gangster costumes, you can find a great deal! If you want to do something a little different, wear a Henley shirt with long baggy trousers and braces. Top it off with a hat and you will have a genuine twenties look.

Learn to dance the Charleston together!

The Charleston was a popular dance that originated in the 1920s during the flapper period. Flappers would dance it at the speakeasies, alone or together, as a way of mocking the "drys," or those who supported Prohibition, as the dance was considered quite immoral and provocative. In fact, it was banned in dancehalls of the day for being too wild!

There are variations and extra steps, but the basic dance is easy to learn. For tips and videos, or tutorials visit: www.charlestondance.co.uk

Why not have a Charleston contest for your guests and award a prize to the winner.

Food and drink

Any cocktail you choose will probably be fitting as the majority of today's cocktails were created in the 1920s to mask the strength and bad taste of bathtub liquors and moonshines. Recipes for drinks popular in the Roaring Twenties include some full of innuendo, like Between the Sheets, or favorites like the Mint Julep or the Old Fashioned. Champagne cocktails were also a big hit. I recommend serving canapés and drinks only. You will most likely want this party to occur in the evening, so people will probably already have had dinner. You can always serve filled bagels as the night wears on, as people need something to soak up the moonshine.

SPEAKEASY CHECKLIST

- Invitations
- Hidden venue
- Password to enter
- A bouncer to do a gun check at the door!
- Art Deco decor
- 1920's slang
- Speakeasy bar
- Tea cups and crystal glasses
- Gangsters and Flappers theme
- Prohibition "bathtub gin" – metal tubs with ice and booze
- Dance and/or listen to jazz
- Do the Charleston
- Award prizes for Best Costume
- Stage a midnight raid by prohibition agents
- Show silent or gangster movies
- Take photos of your guests in costume

SLANG DICTIONARY

Bee's knees	extraordinary thing or idea
Big cheese	the boss
Break it up	stop that, quit the nonsense
Spinach	money
Peepers	eyes
Oysterfruit	pearl
Canary	women singer
Cat's meow	something splendid or stylish
Conk	head
Fuzz	the police
Giggle water	liquor
Gooseberry lay	someone who steals clothes from clothes-lines
Hinky	suspicious
Ice	diamonds
Moll	girlfriend
Ritzy	elegant
Swell	wonderful

Bresaola and Parmesan Crostini

Italian-Americans opened up speakeasies by the thousand and had a tremendous impact on the eating habits of Americans by exposing them to Italian ingredients. They got a taste for Italian food that has never left. If you can't get hold of bresaola, a good parma ham or speck will do just as well.

MAKES 15–20

1 baguette, thinly sliced • olive oil, for brushing • 4 tbsp sunflower oil • 3 tbsp capers
2 large ripe tomatoes • juice of 1 lemon • 2 garlic cloves, peeled and minced
salt and freshly ground black pepper • 100 g/3½ oz bresaola
50 g/1¾ oz Parmesan cheese • Greek basil sprigs, to garnish

Preheat the oven to 180°C/350°F/Gas Mark 4.

To make the crostini, brush both sides of the baguette with olive oil and bake in the oven for 5–6 minutes until crispy. Remove and leave to cool.

Heat the sunflower oil in a small frying pan over a medium heat. Add the capers and they should open like flowers. Once cooked, drain on a plate lined with kitchen paper.

Chop the tomatoes roughly, discarding the seeds and core. Mix the tomatoes, lemon juice, garlic, and salt and pepper together in a bowl.

Put some of the tomato mixture together with a slither of Parmesan, some bresaola and 1 caper on 1 crostini, then garnish with a sprig of basil. Repeat with half of the baked crostinis saving the other half for the Waldorf topping (see p.74).

Waldorf Salad Crostini

Inspired by the luxury New York hotel, the Waldorf Astoria, this legendary salad can be made miniature and is perfect for any speakeasy canapé. You can always substitute the mayonnaise for yogurt for a lighter version, or add chicken if you wish.

MAKES 15–20
4 baby gem lettuces, leaves separated
3 tbsp good-quality mayonnaise
1 tbsp lemon juice
salt and freshly ground black pepper
1 Pink Lady apple, cored and roughly chopped
1 celery stick, thinly sliced
10 red seedless grapes, cut into quarters
50 g/1¾ oz/½ cup walnuts, toasted and chopped
1 small handful of parsley, chopped
baked crostini (see p.73)

Place the baby gem leaves in a large bowl of cold water and leave to soak for 20 minutes until ready to use.

In a medium-sized bowl, whisk together the mayonnaise, lemon juice, salt and pepper. Mix in the apple, celery, grapes, walnuts (reserving some for the garnish) and parsley.

Drain, dry and trim the lettuce leaves to fit the crostini (see p.73). Fill the lettuce with ½ tbsp of the Waldorf mixture and place on top of the crostini. Garnish with the reserved walnuts.

Harissa Chicken Skewers
with Sumac Yogurt Dip

In keeping with the exotic culinary experimentation of the 1920s, tantalise your guests' taste buds
and take on this North African spiced dish.

MAKES 15–20 SKEWERS
4 skinless free-range chicken breasts, cut into bite-sized cubes
2 garlic cloves, peeled and minced • 2 tbsp rose harissa paste
2 red onions, peeled and cut into bite-sized cubes
salt and freshly ground black pepper

FOR THE YOGURT DIPPING SAUCE
170 g/6 oz/¾ cup natural (plain) Greek yogurt
zest of 1 lemon, plus 2 tbsp lemon juice • 1 tbsp sumac, plus a little extra to garnish
30 g/1 oz coriander (cilantro), finely chopped

Place the chicken, garlic and harissa paste in a large non-reactive bowl and
leave to marinate for at least 1 hour, but preferably overnight.

While the chicken is marinating, make the dipping sauce.
Place the yogurt, the lemon zest and juice, sumac and coriander into a bowl and mix well,
then refrigerate until it's ready to serve.

Once the chicken has marinated, soak 20 bamboo skewers in water for 30 minutes,
to prevent them burning during cooking, and preheat the grill to medium-high.

Thread the onion and chicken onto the soaked skewers. Cook under the grill for 4 minutes,
then turn and cook for a further 4 minutes. Finally, take your prepared dipping sauce
from the refrigerator, garnish with a little more sumac, and serve with the skewers.

Halloumi Skewers with Parsley Oil

Bring the Mediterranean to your evening with this little Cypriot number.

MAKES 15–20 SKEWERS

3 tbsp olive oil • 2 garlic cloves, peeled and minced
4 thyme sprigs, finely chopped • salt and freshly ground black pepper
2 aubergines (eggplants), thinly sliced lengthways • 180 g/6½ oz sun-blushed tomatoes
300 g/10½ oz halloumi, cut into bite-sized cubes

FOR THE PARSLEY OIL

juice of 1 lemon • 1 small bunch of parsley, finely chopped • 3 tbsp olive oil

Soak 20 bamboo skewers in water for 30 minutes, to prevent them burning during cooking.

Preheat the grill to medium-high.

In a small bowl, combine the oil, garlic, thyme and salt and pepper and set aside.

Heat a griddle pan over a high heat. Brush both sides of the aubergine slices with the flavoured oil and place on the preheated pan. If the aubergine is looking dry, brush again with the oil to baste. Once cooked, place on a plate and set aside.

Before placing the skewers under the grill, prepare your parsley oil by mixing the lemon juice, parsley and oil together in a small bowl.

Place the tomatoes on kitchen paper to soak up any oil, then thread the aubergine, halloumi and tomato onto the soaked skewers. Place the skewers under the grill until the halloumi starts to sizzle and turn brown (turn appropriately). Once cooked, arrange the skewers on a platter and drizzle with your parsley oil.

Chocolate and Hazelnut Strawberries

Seek out your inner flapper and insist that you get fed under the moonlight by a handsome chap.

SERVES 8–10

2 punnets (cartons) fresh strawberries
200 g/7 oz dark (semisweet) chocolate, roughly chopped
200 g/7 oz white chocolate, finely chopped
50 g/1¾ oz/⅓ cup toasted and chopped hazelnuts

Place a large heatproof bowl over a pan of simmering water, making sure the base of the bowl is not touching the water. Add the dark chocolate and melt, then leave to cool for 5–10 minutes so the chocolate is not too runny.

Cover half of the strawberries in the melted dark chocolate, then sprinkle some with the hazelnuts and leave some plain. Place in the refrigerator until ready to serve.

Repeat with the white chocolate.
When melting the white chocolate, make sure to chop the chocolate finely, and keep the pan of water over a low heat, as it can become grainy when melted on a high heat.

Cocktails

Cocktails, invented to disguise the taste of bootleg liquor, will make any party so much more sophisticated. If you want to be a professional cocktail mixer, then you've got to start somewhere. This "Home Cocktail Starter Pack" contains enough cocktail accessories to help you on your way to a future of drinks mixing.

THE BASIC TOOLS
Boston cocktail shaker • Hawthorne strainer • ice bucket filled with crushed ice • plastic cocktail swords
stirrers • tongs • bar spoons • bar towels • jiggers (measuring cups) • lemon zester
multipurpose bottle opener • sugar syrup (also known as *gomme*)

Minty Fresh

SERVES 1
50 ml/2 fl oz gin or Absolut Citron • 12.5 ml/2½ tsp sugar syrup • 25 ml/1 fl oz/2 tbsp lemon juice
ice • mint leaves, to garnish

Glasses can be either a chilled coupe or a Collins tumbler. If you choose the latter, stack lots
of crushed ice with lemon wedges into the glass with a stem of mint leaves.

Add all the ingredients to the cocktail shaker. Give it a good little shake and fine strain into the glass of
your choosing. Garnish with the mint leaves.

Surrendering Sloe

SERVES 1
50 ml/2 fl oz sloe gin (or 25 ml/1 fl oz/2 tbsp sloe gin and 25ml/1 fl oz/2 tbsp crème de cassis)
12.5 ml/2½ tsp lemon juice • 12.5 ml/2½ tsp sugar syrup • Dom Pérignon Champagne
rose petals or edible gold leaf • ice

Add the liquor, lemon juice and sugar syrup to the shaker. Shake and strain into a chilled glass
and top up with Champagne. Serve with a rose petal or some gold leaf floating on top for
speakeasy decadence.

The Queen of Sheba

"I had 28 costumes in that picture, and if I'd worn them all at once I couldn't have kept warm."
Betty Blythe

Betty Blythe's most famous film is *The Queen of Sheba*. The exoticness of the passion fruit and the bubbles of the Champagne make this drink the jewel in the crown of our cocktails.

SERVES 1

50 ml/2 fl oz sloe gin ✣ squeezed pulp and juice of 2 passion fruit ✣ 12.5 ml/2½ tsp grenadine
12.5 ml/2½ tsp freshly squeezed lime juice ✣ ice ✣ Champagne

Into your cocktail shaker pour the sloe gin, add the pulpy juice of the two passion fruit with its numerous tiny, black seeds, add the grenadine, lime juice and ice.
Shake and strain into a chilled glass and top up with Champagne to make this royal drink last that little bit longer.

Los Angeles Sunset

SERVES 1

25 ml/1 fl oz/2 tbsp freshly squeezed orange juice ✣ dash of sugar syrup or brown sugar
12.5ml/2½ tsp cointreau or triple sec ✣ 35 ml/2½ tbsp brandy
crushed ice ✣ orange and lime slices

Prepare a chilled long stemmed glass or a long fluted glass.

Add all the ingredients to your shaker. Shake and fine strain into your glass and garnish with a slice of orange and lime.

1930's *Cocktail Party*

The stock market has crashed and Betty Blythe has famously lost a huge amount of her fortune. What's a girl to do, when the streets are full of depression, unemployment and soup kitchens? Time for an elegant evening of music, cocktails and canapés. Set a scene of the height of sophistication and party with the rich gentry as it's much more fun! House parties in the 1930s were the entertainment of the day. This was a time when people were listening to the radio for the latest news and yearning for the lavish lifestyles of their favourite movie idols. People partied like they meant it. Guests came to eat, catch up on the local gossip and forget their troubles. Take inspiration from films such as *Gosford Park*, *Atonement* or the legendary Agatha Christie's *Poirot*.

Menu

Watercress, Spinach, Rocket and Roasted Almond Souplette

Baby Leek, Apple and Cheese Tartlets

Roast Duck and Chicory Boats

Bergamot Teacup Crème Caramels

Truffles 3 Ways

Champagne Cocktail

Setting the scene

You could make this part of a full weekend of vintage partying and gather at an English country house for a shooting party reminiscent of the early 1930s. A stunning country mansion full of enough maids and butlers to outnumber the guests would make for a night to be remembered, but, in the real world, simply set the scene in a room with a backdrop of fireplaces, paintings and bookshelves and many regency-style sofas. Light the room with candelabras and style with a few well-placed houseplants. If you think your interior needs a little more period style, play some classic 1930s movies on your flat screen and turn the sound down low.

Invitations

Start with a fascinating guest list and invite your friends to dress up with elegance. The sophistication can start with your invitations. The wonderful, classic style of the formal engraved invite, perfected by the high social classes, will be the most appropriate invitation. All you need is thick cream or white card, a fancy font or your best looping, swirling handwriting.

Music and entertainment

The 1930s was very much the era of the seductive tones of romantic love songs, from artists such as Marlene Dietrich, Ella Fitzgerald or Annette Hanshaw. The famous "Goodnight, Sweetheart" by Al Bowlly is appropriate, as is, of course, the classic Glenn Miller's "Moonlight Serenade". For a bit more fun, download the scores of Hollywood musicals and let Fred Astaire carry you through the night! Or for those who prefer live entertainment, a piano player with singing accompaniment would be perfect.

For a quieter party, lay on a pack of cards and let your guests play Whist for amusement – the board games Monopoly and Scrabble were also hugely popular during this era.

Food and drink

During the 1930s, hosting a full dinner party may have been hard on already strained finances. The recipe books of the period helped hostesses do more with less by offering up stylish dishes that were still relatively inexpensive and easy to put together. Our menu here suggests serving a variety of savoury and sweet canapés with a simple champagne cocktail. For serving, source some silver or glass platters, or simple black and white serving plates.

Create a "drinks station" by placing your drinks for the evening on a low side table. Popular and available alcohol of the time was the forever-loved Champagne, European liquors such as brandy, cognac, gin and whisky, and fortified wines, such as sherry and vermouth. Decant spirits into pretty crystal or cut-glass decanters and serve your guests from them – it's a much more authentic and attractive way to present your drinks. Other essential accessories are an ice bucket, cut-glass, Collins glasses, Martini glasses, old-fashioned champagne coupe (or "saucer") glasses and, perhaps, a soda siphon?

While you are busy welcoming people, guests can then help themselves from the drinks station. Alternatively, and especially if you have a good cocktail maker amongst your group of friends, you can ask one person to be in charge of the drinks. For parties of more than 20, it would be advisable to hire someone to take responsibility for this important part of the evening and find them an outfit, such as a butler's waistcoat or a black and white waitressing dress.

What to wear

Ladies

This is an occasion for luxurious, silky, satin or dark velvet evening dresses, worn floor-skimming or ankle-length. The fashions of the era celebrated the feminine silhouette of the body by means of bias-cutting – look for dresses where the fabric falls into a smooth vertical drape and clings subtly to the body. Evening gowns had very low V-backs or even backless halter-necks, and were often sleeveless. Accessorise with long black gloves, Art Deco jewellery and faux fur stoles or coats. Beige stockings and T-bar shoes or sandals will finish the outfit.

Hair should be dressed neatly. Popular styles were to wave the hair softly around the face. Long hair can be pinned up at the nape of the neck to appear short.

Gentlemen

Fred Astaire should be your inspiration. Men's eveningwear of the 1930s consisted of the double-breasted tuxedo in black or midnight blue; white dinner jackets were also worn, especially in summer. Black ties were worn with tuxedos or dinner jackets. Neat hair is again a must – a short back and sides do is best. Dampen hair down with Bryll cream if possible, and comb over into a side parting.

COCKTAIL PARTY CHECKLIST
- Large county mansion (optional)
- Drawing room-style backdrop
- Elegant "engraved" invitations
- Butler or maid to help serve
- Romantic 1930's music
- Piano entertainment
- Pack of cards/board games
- Candlelight
- Parlour plants
- Cut-glass decanters and glasses
- Champagne saucers
- Serving platters
- Silky floor-length dresses
- Tuxedos

Watercress, Spinach, Rocket and Roasted Almond Souplette

At the outset of the Depression, Al Capone, the notorious gangster from Chicago, established the first soup kitchen. He started it because he wanted to clean up his shady image. Capone's kitchen served three meals a day to ensure that everyone who had lost a job could get a meal. This fresh, invigorating soup certainly wouldn't have been on the menu! This *amuse bouche* is perfectly served in small shot glasses.

Serves 6–8

2 tbsp vegetable oil * 1 tsp caraway seeds * 1 carrot, peeled and finely chopped
1 celery stick, finely chopped * 1 white onion, peeled and finely chopped
1 starchy potato, such as King Edward or Maris Piper, peeled and finely chopped
2 garlic cloves, peeled and roughly chopped * salt and freshly ground black pepper
800 ml/scant 1½ pints/3⅓ cups good-quality chicken stock * 1 tsp caster (superfine) sugar
300 g/10½ oz watercress, spinach and rocket (arugula) salad mix
1 bunch of flat-leaf parsley, roughly chopped
25 g/1 oz/¼ cup toasted flaked (slivered) almonds, plus a little extra to garnish
1 green chilli, deseeded and chopped * 4 tbsp Greek yogurt

Heat the oil in a large saucepan over a medium high heat. Add the caraway seeds, carrot, celery and onion, and cook, stirring continuously, for 3–4 minutes, making sure they do not brown. Add the potato and garlic and cook for a further 2 minutes. Season generously with salt and pepper, then reduce the heat to medium, pour in the chicken stock and sugar and bring to the boil. Reduce the heat to low and simmer for 10 minutes. Once the potato is cooked remove the pan from the heat and leave to cool.

Meanwhile, boil a kettle and pour boiling water over the salad mix and parsley. Drain and cool under cold running water. Place the cooled greens, almonds and chilli into the soup mixture. Transfer the soup to a food processor and purée until smooth. Alternatively, use a hand-held blender. If it's too thick add a little water. Return the soup to the pan, season again if needed, then stir in the yogurt and spoon into individual glasses. The soup should be served lukewarm, so reheat gently if the soup has cooled down completely. Garnish with extra toasted almonds.

Roast Duck and Chicory Boats

Bring decadence to the evening with this duck and fresh orange combination served on a chicory leaf. These glamorous beauties are easy to to put together and you can assemble them at the last minute.

Serves 6–8

320 g/11 oz duck breasts, skin on ● 2 tsp allspice ● 6 tbsp olive oil, plus 1 tbsp for the marinade
salt and freshly ground black pepper ● 4 chicory heads, separated into leaves ● 2 oranges
2 tbsp sherry wine vinegar ● 2 red onions, peeled and finely sliced
1 small bunch of flat-leaf parsley, roughly chopped ● 5 tbsp good-quality chilli jam

Preheat the oven to 190°C/375°F/Gas Mark 5.

First you need to marinate the duck. Place the duck breasts, allspice and 1 tbsp olive oil
into a medium non-reactive bowl and season well. Cover and refrigerate.

Soak the chicory leaves in a bowl of iced water for 10 minutes.

Peel and segment the oranges over a small bowl, making sure to catch all the orange juice
for the dressing. Put the segments to one side and start to make the dressing. Mix the vinegar with
the orange juice and slowly mix in the olive oil. Season well and set aside.

Next, cook the duck in an ovenproof frying pan over a medium-high heat.
Place the duck breasts skin side down and cook for 4–5 minutes, or until the skin is golden brown.
Remember to watch it carefully, as you want to crisp the skin, but don't overcook the meat. After 5 minutes
remove the fat from the pan (do not turn, keep the skin face down) and place the frying pan with the duck
breasts into the oven. Cook for a further 12 minutes, or until the duck is medium rare. Place the duck breast
on a plate and leave to rest for 5 minutes.

While the duck is resting, place the orange segments, onions, parsley and dressing in a bowl and mix
together thoroughly. Thinly slice the duck breast. To assemble, place a slice of duck breast,
½ tsp chilli jam and a small amount of the orange salad on a leaf of chicory.

Baby Leek, Apple and Cheese Tartlets

These delicious savoury tartlets make for a very pretty canapé to pass around your guests or serve as a light lunch dish, with a green leaf salad. The filo tartlet cases can be made ahead, but they are best served warm, so the pastry remains crisp.

Makes 12

375 g/13 oz ready-rolled puff pastry ❋ plain (all-purpose) flour, for dusting
275 g/9¾ oz baby leeks ❋ 120 g/4/12 oz Soignon goat's cheese ❋ 2 Pink Lady apples
50 g/1¾ oz/½ cup Cheddar cheese, grated ❋ 3 thyme sprigs ❋ 1 egg, lightly beaten

Preheat the oven to 200°C/400°F/Gas Mark 6.

Place the ready rolled pastry on a floured surface and roll out slightly. Using a 7 cm/2¾ in round cookie cutter, stamp out 12 circles and arrange on a lined baking tray. Using the tip of a sharp knife, mark a border inside each one, about 0.5cm/¼ in from the edge, or use a 6 cm/2½ in round cookie cutter to stamp out an inner circle. Place in the refrigerator and leave for 20 minutes.

Meanwhile, trim the baby leeks and slice. Cut the goat's cheese into 14 slices, discarding the 2 waxy end slices, and core the apples, then cut into quarters and slice crossways. Remove the pastry rounds from the refrigerator and place a round of goat's cheese on the pastry. Place 3 slices of apple on top and a couple of sliced leeks. Garnish with the grated Cheddar cheese and thyme. Using a pastry brush, coat the border with the beaten egg and bake for 15–20 minutes until the pastry is crisp and golden.

Bergamot Teacup Crème Caramel

A marriage of French and Chinese flavours, with the lushness of both bergamot and caramel combined into one rich dessert... what's not to love?

SERVES 6–8 DEPENDING ON TEACUP SIZE
300 g/10½ oz/1½ cups caster (superfine) sugar ● 150 ml/5 fl oz/⅔ cup water

FOR THE CUSTARD
4 Earl Grey tea bags ● 320 ml/11 fl oz/scant 1½ cups full fat milk
360 ml/12½ fl oz/generous 1½ cups double (heavy) cream
½ tsp vanilla extract ● 1 large egg, plus 4 yolks
60 g/2¼ oz/scant ⅓ cup caster (superfine) sugar

FOR THE TOPPING
50 ml/1¾ fl oz/scant ¼ cup maple syrup

Preheat the oven to 150°C/300°F/Gas Mark 2. Lightly grease 6–8 teacups with a neutral-tasting oil.

To make the caramel, place the sugar and water in a small saucepan over a low heat and stir until the sugar has dissolved. Bring to the boil and cook for 10–12 minutes, or until golden. Pour the mixture into the prepared teacups and tilt them in a circular motion, making sure that the caramel covers the sides of the cup, but being careful not to burn your fingers. Set aside and leave the caramel to set.

Next, make the custard. Place the tea bags, milk, cream and vanilla extract into a heavy-based saucepan and cook over a medium heat, allowing it to gently come to the boil. In a separate bowl, place the eggs, egg yolks and sugar in a bowl and whisk until it is evenly combined. Remove the tea bags from the milk, wringing them out for an enhanced flavour, and gradually add to the egg mixture, gently stirring with a spoon to combine, making sure not to create a foamy consistency. Carefully pour the custard into the cups. If the mixture is a little lumpy pass through a sieve.

Place the teacups in a deep baking dish and carefully pour in enough hot water to submerge the cups halfway. Bake for 35–40 minutes, or until set. Remove the cups from the baking dish and refrigerate until completely cold. To finish, spoon over ½ tbsp of maple syrup.

Truffles 3 Ways

The 1930s saw a surge in the chocolate market – well-known confectionary brands were establishing themselves in this period. Try making these sensational chocolate truffles as a delectable finale to any evening – they're so delicious that no one will guess how quick and easy they are to make.

MAKES ABOUT 15 OF EACH TRUFFLE, ABOUT 45 IN TOTAL

300 g/10½ oz good-quality dark (semisweet) chocolate (at least 70% cocoa solids)
90 ml/3 fl oz/⅓ cup double (heavy) cream ✽ 150 g/5½ oz/ scant ¾ cup (11 tbsp) unsalted butter
150 g/5½ oz/1½ cups (unsweetened) cocoa powder, sifted

FOR THE GINGER TRUFFLES
2 tbsp glacé (candied) ginger, roughly chopped ✽ glacé (candied) ginger, to decorate

FOR THE SALTED CARAMEL TRUFFLES
1 tsp Maldon sea salt ✽ 1 tbsp dulce leche ✽ 1 Dime bar, chopped ✽ salt, to decorate

FOR THE ROSE TRUFFLES
1 tsp rose essence ✽ dried rose petals, to decorate

Place 100 g/3½ oz of the chocolate and 2 tbsp of the cream into a heatproof bowl and place the bowl over a pan of gently simmering water (making sure the base does not touch the bottom of the bowl). Heat the chocolate until it is completely melted. Remove from the heat, add the ingredients of one of the flavours, and mix well. Place the mixture in a small airtight container and chill in the refrigerator for 6–8 hours, or until firm.

When the truffle mixture is the desired consistency scoop out the mixture with a teaspoon and roll into truffle size balls.

Finally, place the truffles in a tin lined with non-stick baking parchment and cover with cling film and put back into the refrigerator. Repeat the same method for the other flavours. Once you have made 3 batches of truffles sift the cocoa powder onto a large plate and coat all the truffles in the cocoa, then decorate.

Champagne Cocktail

"I had taken two finger-bowls of Champagne, and the scene had changed before my eyes into something significant, elemental and profound."

F. Scott Fitzgerald

Add a touch of the finest black raspberry liqueur to create an exquisite glass of sparkling magic.

SERVES 1
8 ml/1½ tsp Chambord liqueur ✳ Champagne
raspberries, blackberries or blueberries, for garnish

Add the Chambord liqueur to a champagne flute or saucer and top with Champagne, to taste.
Add a raspberry or blackberry or blueberry, to garnish.

A 1940's Picnic

Shove that under your feet," he observed to the Mole,
as he passed it down into the boat.
"What's inside it?" asked the Mole, wriggling with curiosity.
"There's cold chicken inside it," replied the Rat briefly;
"coldtonguecoldhamcoldbeefpickledgherkinssaladfrenchrolls-
cresssandwichespottedmeatgingerbeerlemonadesodawater—"
"O stop, stop!" cried the Mole in ecstasies:
"This is too much!"
The Wind in the Willows, Kenneth Grahame

Picnics are as old as time, from the days of the pilgrims to Georgian outdoor feasts in pleasure gardens; from the escapism and picknickery-nicknackery of the Victorians, who still made a rather formal affair of the occasion, to today's simple picnics which have taken inspiration in deep-rooted literary tales from *Wind in the Willows* or the great adventures of the *Famous Five* and their mouthwatering picnic packages; picnics have always been with us. When the weather is swell and you have emptied the pantry of goodies, pack everything up and off you go outside to enjoy the sunshine and the company of your sweetheart.

MENU

Fiery Ginger Beer

Homemade Lemonade

Potted Parsley Beef

Baguette and Butter

Pickles

Chervil and Spring Onion
Potato Salad

Lemon Drizzle Squares

Plum Frangipane Tart

Setting the scene

Drive out to country in your jalopy, take a bus trip or simply enjoy a good walk to find the perfect spot under a tree or on a costal path. Spread a blanket or tablecloth on the ground, take along a thermos, bottled drinks, fresh bread and simple lunch food and you have the makings of a lovely warm afternoon outing.

Picnic hampers from the 1940s

For a real retro delight, invest in a hamper of the decade. These very practical picnic hampers can be found in immaculate condition with wonderful compartments inside, with enamelled food containers and everything you need to use safely contained in one place. You can find them online or try charity shops and antique markets.

A hamper is not essential, but do not turn up with plastic bags! In addition to a simple basket, you could also use old suitcases to transport everything. Put dry goods in one and food and drink in another. You will need an eager beaver to assist with transporting what you need for a larger picnic.

Dress for the day

It should be a sunny day for your picnic, so choose
the perfect dress to spend the day in. Think about how
comfortable the dress is to sit down in – anything tight
around the waist is bad news for digestion – and don't
choose anything too short – the chaps don't need a flash
of your undergarments whilst enjoying their eats.

Pretty tea dresses with cardigans, high-waisted shorts or
knee length skirts, sensible flat- or block-heeled shoes
and square-shouldered jackets recalling the cut of wartime
uniforms make for a great nod to the 1940's experience.

Lay down your trilby's guys – a white shirt on top of a white
vest, with sleeves rolled up, is a perfect way to take a rest
from wearing full suits. For a more relaxed look, add a
knitted vest, corduroys and braces, and you will be set
up for frolicking in the sunshine.

Don't forget the blanket!

Sometimes it does help to be a little prepared. So here are
Betty Blythe's tips to be ever-ready for a perfect picnic:

Before packing, cut food into portions so it is easier to serve.

For vintage appeal wrap your food into waxed paper tied
with twine.

A picnic can be ruined by thoughtless packaging, choose
foods that are easy to transport and if in doubt – leave it out!

If you don't have a complete picnic set, don't forget to check
you have plates, cups, cutlery and napkins. Disposable items
are a good idea.

Taking bottles of giggle water? Don't be a Dumb Dora
and remember that bottle opener!

Bring a basket to store cameras, video camcorders
and sunscreen.

A bag to clear your rubbish into, paper towels, hand
wipes and tea towels for the end of picnic clear up.

Even if it was delectable, throw away any perishable
food that has been left out for more than a few hours.

Take some insect repellent to make sure you have
a bite-free time!

Bring a blanket or cloth to cover the things you don't want
to show when taking memorable photos.

Beverages

No cans please! Instead, choose sodas in vintage-style bottles. Use a funnel to decant beverages into plain bottles with stoppers or use Sherry or wine bottles with corks. Take a pitcher for juice, lemonade or iced tea. Remember that bottles with ceramic stoppers can be cleaned and re-used year after year.

For cool drinks try a refreshing lemonade or ginger beer. Much needed after all that exhilaration from walking in the countryside to find that perfect picnic spot.

Remember all this and you will have a gas!

PICNIC CHECKLIST
- Good weather
- Thoughtful destination
- 1940's outfits
- Blanket
- Hamper, baskets or suitcases
- Cutlery
- Vintage bottles
- Food and drink
- Bottle opener
- End of picnic clear-up kit
- Picnic games

Games

If you've finished daydreaming and whispering sweet nothings into your doll's ear, taking games to your picnic is a great idea. For retro appeal, think a pack of cards, dominos, or pickup sticks, or, if you want to enjoy really old fashioned lawn games: boules, quoits, croquet and a badminton set is key to an afternoon well spent with a larger group.

Homemade Lemonade

We have the Egyptians to thank for creating this drink more than 1,500 years ago.
This essential summer drink is the perfect way to cool down on a summer's day.

SERVES 6–8

200 g/7 oz/1 cup golden caster (superfine) sugar ❋ 240 ml/8½ fl oz/generous 1 cup water
240 ml/8½ fl oz/generous 1 cup fresh lemon juice (juice of about 6–7 lemons)
thickly pared zest of 2 lemons
800 ml–1 litre/1¼–1⅔ pints/3⅓–4 cups cold water

First make the syrup. Heat the sugar and the 240 ml/8½ fl oz/generous 1 cup water
in a small saucepan and stir until the sugar has dissolved. Once the syrup is completely
clear, juice your lemons and pour into a large jug.

Next, pour the sugar syrup together with the lemon juice into glass bottles with a seal.
Finish off by placing lemon peels inside the bottle. At your picnic, dilute with the cold water.

Fiery Ginger Beer

First made as an alcoholic beverage in Great Britain in the 1700s, ginger beer has remained a stout favourite, despite becoming a soft drink. Fiery and bubbly, absolutely spiffing! No picnic is complete without it. Try adding a little shot of spiced rum for an extra zing.

SERVES 6–8
80 g/2¾ oz/scant ½ cup muscovado (soft brown) sugar
200 g/7 oz fresh root ginger, peeled ❋ 4 limes
1–1.5 litres/1¾–2½ pints/4–6⅓ cups sparkling mineral water
1 bunch of mint ❋ 1 bottle of dark rum (optional)

Place the sugar in a large bowl and, using a cheese grater, coarsely grate the ginger over the sugar. Remove the rind from 3 of your limes with a vegetable peeler and add to the bowl, then using a rolling pin, crush the ginger, lime and sugar mixture for 20 seconds to release the flavours. Squeeze the juice from 3 limes into the mixture and stir well. You may want to add a little more sugar or lime juice at this point. Pass the mixture through a sieve and transfer into 3 glass bottles with a lid.

Pack the bottles in your picnic basket. When ready to serve fill the bottle up with the sparkling water and a couple sprigs of mint. To spice things up, add a shot of rum to your glass.

Chervil and Spring Onion Potato Salad

I adore potato salad and it does seem to make an appearance at many occasions. It is such a simple and deliciously practical food to take to the great outdoors. In this recipe add chervil – a pretty little herb – for a mild, sweet aniseed flavour.

SERVES 6–8

1 kg/2 lb 4 oz salad potatoes, such as Vivaldi, cut into quarters
salt and freshly ground black pepper
170 g/6 oz/¾ cup natural (plain) Greek yogurt
150 g/5½ oz salad cream ❋ 3 tbsp white wine vinegar
2 tbsp Dijon mustard ❋ 2 tbsp cornichon vinegar, from the cornichon jar
1 bunch of spring onions (scallions), trimmed and sliced
2 celery sticks, sliced on an angle ❋ ½ bunch of chervil, chopped
1 small bunch of flat-leaf parsley, chopped ❋ 80 g/2¾ oz cornichons, sliced

Cook the potatoes in a large saucepan of boiling salted water for about 8–10 minutes until tender.
Make sure not to overcook as they will become mushy in the salad.
Drain and cool by pouring cold water over them.

In a small bowl, mix together the yogurt, salad cream, vinegar, Dijon mustard and cornichon vinegar.
Pour over the potatoes, season well and gently mix. It is fine that the potatoes are still slightly
warm – the flavour will absorb better when they are a little warm.
Add the remaining ingredients and refrigerate before use.

Potted Parsley Beef

Potting has been with us for centuries as a thrifty ways to turn leftovers, excesses and cheap cuts into delicious snacking food, and to extend their shelf life. Perfect picnic food, pick up a fresh baguette on your way to the picnic spot and accompany with little jars of pickles and a light salad.

SERVES 6–8

150 g/5½ oz/10 tbsp salted butter ❋ ½ tsp ground ginger
½ tsp ground mace or nutmeg ❋ 3 garlic cloves, peeled and minced
large pinch of cayenne pepper ❋ salt and freshly ground black pepper
500 g/1 lb 2 oz braising steak, fat and sinew removed
1 small bunch of flat-leaf parsley, roughly chopped

Preheat the oven to 150°C/300°F/Gas Mark 2.

Place a small saucepan over a low heat and melt the butter with the ginger, mace, garlic, cayenne and salt and pepper to taste. Do this slowly so the garlic does not burn.

Cut the beef into large chunks and place in an ovenproof dish with a tight-fitting lid.
Pour the butter mixture over the beef and cook in the oven for 4–5 hours, or until very soft (you could even leave it in the oven overnight). Check the beef after 2 hours and turn the pieces over. Cover again and return to the oven for the remaining time. Once the beef is done remove the lid and, using a fork, flake the beef, if it is still a little firm return to the oven for a further 30 minutes. Leave to cool.

Stir the parsley into the steak and transfer to glass pots.
Serve with a chunk of fresh bread and potato salad.

Lemon Drizzle Squares

An all-time favourite and delicious with a cup of earl grey tea. Unwrap this light lemony
sponge to bring sunshine to any picnic.

SERVES 6–8

FOR THE CRUST

170 g/6 oz/¾ cup butter, at room temperature, plus extra for greasing
75 g/2¾ oz/¼ cup + 2 tbsp granulated sugar
195 g/scant 7 oz/generous 1⅓ cups plain (all-purpose) flour,
plus extra for dusting ❋ pinch of salt

FOR THE FILLING

4 large eggs ❋ 400 g/14 oz/2 cups granulated sugar
1½ tbsp grated lemon zest (4–6 lemons)
180 ml/6½ fl oz/generous ¾ cup freshly squeezed lemon juice
90 g/3¼ oz/scant ⅔ cup plain (all-purpose) flour

Preheat the oven to 180°C/350°F/Gas Mark 4. Grease and line a 25 x 25 cm/10 x 10 in square
tin with baking parchment.

For the crust, using an electric mixer, cream the butter and sugar until light and fluffy.
Combine the flour and salt and, with the mixer on low, add to the butter until just mixed.
Place the dough on a well-floured surface and gather into a ball. If the dough is too soft at this stage
refrigerate for 20 minutes. Flatten the dough with floured hands and press it into the prepared tin.
Press the dough 2.5 cm/1 in up the sides of the tin and bake for 15–20 minutes until very lightly browned.
Leave to cool on a wire rack. Leave the oven on.

For the filling, whisk together the eggs, sugar, lemon zest, lemon juice and flour. Pour into the crust
and bake for 30–35 minutes until the filling is set. Leave to cool at room temperature.

Take the tin whole to your picnic or slice into small squares, individually
wrapping each in baking parchment.

Plum Frangipane Tart

Sweet, juicy plums and a delicate taste of almonds is a sure-fire way to get into your sweethearts arms! This versatile tart can follow the seasons, the plums can be replaced with other stone fruits such as cherries or apricots in summer. And in winter you can use apples or pears, although don't think you will be taking it outdoors – have an indoor picnic instead.

SERVES 6–8

FOR THE PASTRY (PIE DOUGH)
185 g/6½ oz/1⅓ cups plain (all-purpose) flour, plus extra for dusting
100 g/3½ oz/7 tbsp butter, cut into cubes
1 medium egg yolk ● ¾ tsp salt ● 2½ tbsp cold water

FOR THE FRANGIPANE
200 g/7 oz/scant 1 cup unsalted butter ● 200 g/7 oz/1 cup caster (superfine) sugar
200 g/7 oz/2¼ cups ground almonds ● 2 eggs, lightly beaten
1 medium egg yolk ● 2 tbsp plain (all-purpose) flour
6 ripe plums, stoned (pitted) and quartered
20 g/¾ oz/scant ¼ cup toasted hazelnuts, roughly chopped

For the pastry, put the flour into a bowl, add the butter and rub it in with your fingertips until it resembles fine breadcrumbs. Beat the egg yolk, salt and cold water together and mix into the flour butter mixture to bring the pastry together. Knead lightly and chill for 30 minutes.

For the frangipane, using an electric mixer, mix the butter, sugar, almonds, eggs, egg yolk and flour together until smooth.

Preheat the oven to 180°C/350°F/Gas Mark 4.

Roll out the chilled dough thinly on a floured work surface and use it to line a 25 cm/10 in tart ring. Trim away any excess pastry. Spoon the frangipane into the tart case so that it comes three-quarters up the sides. Smooth over the surface with a spatula and cover the frangipane evenly with the plums, then scatter over the hazelnuts. Bake in the oven for 30–40 minutes, or until the pastry is crisp and golden brown and the fruit is tender.

1950's Street Party

A grand gala tea party this one. This event is appropriate for the whole family, or, if you fancy, the whole street – what afternoon wouldn't be well spent in the company of young and old? Children will love the colourfulness of this utterly traditional setting, grandparents can enjoy a nice sit down at a table filled with treats from their childhoods, and everyone can enjoy rocking and rolling to the sounds of Buddy Holly!

The tradition of street parties has a long history as a popular way of celebrating special days. Many were organised to mark the end of WWI and since that time the community get-together has grown in popularity. The Coronation of Queen Elizabeth II in 1953 and the Silver Jubilee in 1977 were notable occasions that brought communities onto the streets to celebrate. They continue to be organised for major days of celebration and are an excellent way to get all the neighbours together in the summer. Here is all you need to know about putting on your own 1950's-style street party.

MENU

Spiced Sausage Rolls

Asparagus and Bacon Quiche

Coronation Chicken Buns

The Sweetest Jam Tarts

Mango and Passion Fruit
Pavlova

Elderflower and Raspberry Jelly

Pimms Punch

How to organise a street party

Street parties can be fun to organise and a great way of discovering your community spirit. It's worth getting the ball rolling a couple of months in advance before you want it to be held. You can start by inviting everyone in your street to a meeting to plan the event and asking your council about road closures. It's important that everyone feels involved in the event, and shares the jobs that need to be done.

A week before, send out a reminder for the party and the need to move cars off the street. Display the legal order for the road closure. On the day, set up the road closure signs and it's time to set the scene!

Alternatively, create a private party with friends and family – a small wedding party, a child's birthday party or a special anniversary – and hold it in the style of a street party in your own garden.

Set the scene

Set up long stretches of oblong trestle tables covered with white tablecloths and a gathering of wooden chairs straight from the houses of the street (or an eclectic mix from friends and family), to form a simple backdrop for your street party. Time to colour it up: choose a theme and try to stick to it for a chic effect. Alternatively, welcome a collection of everyone's leftover party pieces and it will have the charm of being completely eclectic.

It's a fabulous time for crafting your own decorations: bunting, paper chains, lanterns and balloons are all perfect. If you feel a little patriotic, adorn your scene with national flags and vintage memorabilia such as biscuit tins and mugs – these can be found at local bric-a-brac stalls or by rummaging in your granny's attic.

Decorations

Bunting

Bunting was originally a specific type of lightweight wool fabric manufactured from the turn of the 17th century and was used for making ribbons. Now, bunting is used especially for street parties and flags including signal flags for the Royal Navy. We are lucky that bunting is so very popular now – it is available in the most unexpected places and in various lovely designs!

But… bunting is so easy and fun to make and can be made from absolutely anything: from scraps of fabric or old clothing to empty cereal boxes and even plastic bags.

To make bunting you will need:
- Scissors
- Needle and thread/stapler/glue
- Fabric/coloured plastic/cereal boxes or any source material you like
- Thin rope or tape
- Sequins/buttons/glitter or any other decorative items

All you need is to do is cut out triangles or squares of the materials you want to use, then sew, tie, staple or glue the triangle shapes onto thin rope or tape. You can also make your bunting more decorative by adding paint, sequins, buttons or anything else you like.

Tie the bunting from side to side across the road, between lamp posts, drainpipes, upstairs windows and trees.

Table settings

The fun thing about a street party is that is that everyone who comes can bring something of their own to the table, but there are a few necessary items:

- Trestle table and mismatched chairs
- White tablecloths
- Crockery – look for retro designs and colours, polka dots, block colour and shaped plates.
- Cake stands or platters
- Coloured glasses/tumblers
- Straws
- Jugs for drinks
- Plastic trays to carry things
- Stainless steel or robust plastic cutlery
- Patterned disposable or material napkins

Music

Rock 'n' roll started in the early fifties and completely revolutionised musical tastes, especially amongst young people. Such feel-good music will add a great backdrop to this kind of party – you can start off with playing it subtly in the background and turn it up later for a bit of dancing. For large parties hire a DJ and sound kit, but for modest gatherings purchase compilations from the internet and your party will sure swing! Perhaps if you raid your family attic you will find a record player and some fifties records – look for Elvis Priestly, Chuck Berry and Johnny Cash.

Food and drink

Most street parties occurred during times of austerity so food would have been simple and consisted of whatever was available. Buffet food from the 1950s included delights containing Spam, cocktail sausages, liverwurst pate, smoked salmon canapés, ritz biscuits, tutti fruiti and, of course, the good old jam sandwich. Nowadays we have endless delights to choose from, so I have suggested some modernised and colourful, celebration-worthy recipes (without Spam!) for you to make.

If you are asking others to contribute to the buffet, other dishes that are suitable for street parties include crudités and dips, sandwiches, scotch eggs, trifles and the classic jelly and ice-cream.

1953 saw the end of sweet rationing, yippee! What better excuse for sweets in paper bags? Create a retro sweetie bag for the children and grownups to take away at the end of the party. Fill with blackjacks, fruit salads, sherbert fountains with a stick of liquorice, raspberry drops, liquorice allsorts, dolly mixtures, gobstoppers, sherbet lemons and toffees.

Games

There's plenty more fun to be had! Use chalks to draw on the pavement to play hopscotch, or you can try out hula hooping. For those who want a more relaxing time, how about creating a tombola to play or starting a game of bingo?

What to wear

Ladies

The 1950s was the decade of the hourglass figure with its nipped-in waistline. A time of the most girlie femininity, think floral patterns and novelty prints, bows, frills, circle skirts, layers of petticoats and ankle-length bobby socks. Daywear would have also included brightly coloured Capri pants, exquisitely detailed twin-sets and halterneck dresses. High peep-toe heels were the shoes to be seen in the start of the decade, followed by kitten heels, or mid-height strappy sandals by the mid-fifties. Hair could be pulled back in ponytails or worn in big curls. Take inspiration from Marilyn Monroe.

Men

Look to Buddy Holly or James Dean; rock 'n' roll or rockabilly. Slim-fitting shirts, thin ties, rolled-up sleeves, and chunky specs. Fifties mens' shoes include winklepickers, chelsea boots, loafers, creepers, and more. The fifties also saw the "Grease" look – teddy boys made their mark with jeans, leather jackets and white t-shirts.

STREET PARTY CHECKLIST

- Invites or meeting with neighbours
- Cars moved or gardens cleared
- Trestle tables
- Chairs for everyone
- White tablecloths
- Bunting and decorations
- Retro tableware
- Retro food
- Music and equipment
- 50's records
- Pack of chalk
- Hula hoops
- Bows and frills
- Twinsets
- Peeptoes
- White t-shirts, blue jeans, leather jackets
- Winklepickers
- Bryll cream

Spiced Sausage Rolls

Sausage rolls are the best party food ever – no buffet would be complete without this original street party favourite. Make sure you eat one before they all go!

MAKES 20

2 garlic cloves, peeled and crushed ❋ 1 small white onion, peeled and finely chopped
2 tbsp finely chopped parsley ❋ 2 tbsp finely chopped oregano
finely grated zest of 1 lemon ❋ 2 red chillies, deseeded and chopped
450 g/1 lb sausage meat ❋ 75 ml/2¾ fl oz/5 tbsp water
75 g/2¾ oz roasted red peppers, finely chopped ❋ 1 tsp ground cumin
2 tsp ground coriander ❋ salt and freshly ground black pepper
1 x 375 g/13 oz packet ready-rolled puff pastry ❋ plain (all-purpose) flour, for dusting
1 beaten egg, for glazing ❋ 2 tbsp sesame seeds ❋ tomato relish or mustard, to serve

Preheat the oven to 200°C/400°F/Gas Mark 6.

Place the garlic, onion, herbs, lemon zest, chillies and sausage meat in a food processor with the water and blend until fairly smooth. Transfer the mixture to a mixing bowl and stir in the peppers, cumin and coriander and season well.

Unroll the pastry onto a well-floured surface and slice the pastry in half lengthways. Divide the sausage mixture in half and spread along the length of each pastry strip in a cylinder shape, leaving a 1 cm/½ in edge. Tightly roll the pastry around the sausage meat and brush the ends with a little beaten egg to secure. Use a sharp serrated knife to cut each roll into 10 pieces, each about 2.5 cm/1 in long, and place on a large baking sheet. Brush more beaten egg all over the pastry. Sprinkle over the sesame seeds and bake for 25–35 minutes, or until the pastry is puffed and crisp and the meat has cooked through.

Remove from the oven and eat hot or cold with some tomato relish or mustard.

Asparagus and Bacon Quiche

Your splendid buffet is made all the better for the arrival of this perfect quiche. Serve fresh from the oven, but it's also enjoyable cold, served with green salad. Asparagus can be replaced with broccoli if you fancy.

SERVES 6–8

375 g/13 oz shortcrust pastry (flaky pie dough) ❋ plain (all-purpose) flour, for dusting
100 g/3½ oz asparagus tips ❋ 1 tbsp olive oil
180 g/6½ oz bacon lardons (small pieces) ❋ 1 large leek, trimmed and finely sliced
2 large eggs, plus 2 large egg yolks ❋ 200 ml/7 fl oz/¾ cup double (heavy) cream
60 g/2¼ oz/½ cup Cheddar cheese, finely grated
60 g/2¼ oz/½ cup Gruyère cheese, finely grated
2 tbsp roughly chopped tarragon ❋ 2 tbsp roughly chopped parsley
salt and freshly ground black pepper, to taste

Preheat the oven to 180°C/350°F/Gas Mark 4.

Roll the pastry out on a lightly floured work surface and use to line a 35 x 11 cm/14 x 4¼ in fluted rectangular loose-bottomed tin. Place in the freezer for 10–15 minutes to stop the pastry from shrinking. Remove the pastry from the freezer and cover with baking parchment. Fill with baking beans and blind bake for 10 minutes. Remove the parchment paper and beans and return to the oven for a further 5 minutes.

In the meantime, blanch the asparagus for 1 minute in a pan of boiling water, then rinse under cold water and set aside.

Heat the oil in a frying pan and cook the lardons for 5–6 minutes, or until crispy. Remove with a slotted spoon and drain on kitchen paper. Add the leeks to the pan and sweat gently for 10–12 minutes until softened.

Meanwhile, whisk the eggs and yolks in a large bowl. Add the cream, lardons, leeks, cheese, tarragon, parsley, salt and pepper and mix well. Pour the mixture into the pre-baked tart tin and top with the asparagus. Bake for 25–30 minutes, or until cooked through.

Remove the tart from the oven and serve warm or cold.

Coronation Chicken Buns

This fabulous dish was created for Elizabeth II's coronation in 1953 and has been a classic ever since. Best made the day before to let the flavours truly infuse. A great sandwich filling, it's also good on jacket potatoes.

SERVES 6–8

4 free-range skinless chicken breasts ❊ 1 cinnamon stick
1 tsp coriander seeds ❊ 2 dried red chillies ❊ 5 black peppercorns ❊ 2 pinches saffron threads
2 bay leaves ❊ 6 cm/2½ in piece fresh root ginger, peeled ❊ 2 tbsp curry powder
5 tbsp good-quality mango chutney ❊ 50 g/1¾ oz/generous ¼ cup dried apricots, finely chopped
2 tsp Worcestershire sauce ❊ 50 g/1¾ oz/½ cup flaked (slivered) almonds, toasted
grated zest and juice of 1 lemon ❊ 200 g/7 oz/¾ cup natural (plain) Greek yogurt
salt and freshly ground black pepper ❊ 1 large bunch of coriander (cilantro), roughly chopped
16 snack rolls, wholegrain and white ❊ 100 g/3½ oz mixed salad leaves

Put the chicken in a large pan together with the cinnamon, coriander seeds, chillies, peppercorns, saffron, bay leaves and half of the ginger. Fill the pan with cold water until all the chicken breasts are covered, then cover with a lid and bring to the boil. Reduce the heat to low and gently simmer for about 1 hour. Remove the pan from the heat and leave to cool. Remove the chicken from the water while the chicken is still slightly warm and flatten the breast with a rolling pin and pull apart.

Finely chop the rest of the ginger and place in a large bowl. Toast the curry powder in a dry frying pan until fragrant and add to the ginger together with the mango chutney, apricots, Worcestershire sauce, flaked almonds, lemon zest and juice, yogurt and salt and pepper. Mix well and gently stir in the chicken. Leave to chill in the refrigerator for 2–3 hours, or overnight.

Just before serving add the chopped coriander to the chicken mixture. To assemble the buns place a few salad leaves and 1 heaped tbsp of the Coronation chicken in the buns. Enjoy!

The Sweetest Jam Tarts

Be the queen of hearts and bake some tarts, and your guests will steal them away! If you want to involve the children, these simple tarts will be sure to please – get them to cut out the pastry, spoon in the jam and, when cooked, bring them to the table in vintage tins.

Makes 24
225 g/8 oz/scant 1⅔ cups plain (all-purpose) flour, plus extra for dusting
¼ tsp salt ✿ 25 g/1 oz/2 tbsp golden caster (superfine) sugar
150 g/5½ oz/2⅔ cup unsalted butter, softened, plus extra for greasing
1 medium egg yolk ✿ 25 ml/1 fl oz/scant 2 tbsp cold water

FOR THE FILLING
Blueberry jam ✿ Strawberry jam ✿ Apricot jam

Mix the flour, salt, sugar and butter together in a bowl.
Rub the mixture between your fingers until the mixture resembles large breadcrumbs.
Add the egg yolk and water, bit by bit, and knead the pastry gently to form a ball.
Cover with cling film and place in the refrigerator for about 1 hour.

Preheat the oven to 200°C/400°F/Gas Mark 6. Grease 2 x 12-hole shallow tart tins.

Roll out the pastry on a lightly floured surface until it is about 3–4 mm/⅛–⅙ in thick.
Using a large cup or pastry cutter, cut out circles and place into each hole of the tart tins, pressing the edges of the pastry lightly into the hole. Fill each tart with about 2 heaped tsp of jam.
Alternate between the different jams to have some variation. Bake for about 15–20 minutes, or until the pastry is golden. Cool on a wire rack.

Serve warm or cold.

Elderflower and Raspberry Jelly

Put some sparkle into your party by using sparkling elderflower to make this elegant party classic. Make sure you make this the day before for the best results. You can purchase vintage jelly moulds – look in the back of relatives' kitchen cupboards, online or in bric-a-brac shops.

SERVES 6–8

1 tbsp sunflower oil ❊ 8 gelatine leaves ❊ 4 tbsp water
750 ml/1¼ pints/3 cups sparkling elderflower pressé
90 g/3¼ oz/¾ cup fresh raspberries

FOR THE RASPBERRY JELLY

225 g/8 oz/1⅛ cups caster (superfine) sugar ❊ 500 ml/17 fl oz/generous 2 cups water
300 g/10½ oz/scant 2½ cups raspberries ❊ 7 leaves gelatine

Oil 3–4 jelly moulds with the oil and set aside until ready to use.

Place the 8 gelatine leaves in a small heatproof bowl, add the water and leave to soak for 10 minutes, or until the gelatine is very soft. Place the bowl over a pan of barely simmering water and stir until the gelatine has completely dissolved. Add the gelatine to the jug of elderflower pressé and stir well. Fill half of the prepared jelly moulds with the elderflower mixture, leaving room for the second layer of raspberry jelly. Depending on the size of the mould, place in the refrigerator for 1–2 hours until set.

After the first setting time press the 90 g/3¼ oz/¾ cup raspberries into the elderflower jelly, making sure that they are at the bottom of the jelly mixture. You must first let the mixture set a little so the raspberries do not float to the top. Leave to set for a further 2–3 hours.

Once the elderflower layer has set, make the raspberry jelly. Heat the sugar, the 500 ml/17 fl oz/generous 2 cups water and the 300 g/10½ oz/scant 2½ cups raspberries in a pan until the sugar has dissolved. Stir well to break down the raspberries, then remove from the heat and whiz in a blender. Strain the raspberry mixture through a fine sieve into a clean pan, then heat gently over a low heat until warm. Remove the pan from the heat.

Soak the 7 gelatine leaves in a small bowl of cold water until softened. Take the gelatine out of the water and squeeze out excess water. Stir the gelatine into the raspberry mixture and leave to cool. Once the mixture has cooled, pour on top of the elderflower jelly and chill overnight to set completely.

Mango and Passion Fruit Pavlova

In the March of 1953, eggs were taken off the ration, and then, in April, real cream became available...
Thank goodness, because we wouldn't like to make this pavlova without them! Passion fruit and mango
have brought this heavenly dessert up to date, but soft summer fruits are just as delicious.

SERVES 8–10

8 egg whites ❋ 400 g/14 oz/ 2 cups golden caster (superfine) sugar
2 tsp white vinegar ❋ 6 passion fruit, pulp removed
2 ripe Alfonso mangoes, peeled and sliced into thin slithers
600 ml/1 pint/2½ cups double (heavy) cream ❋ 3 mint sprigs

Preheat the oven to 140°C/275°F/Gas Mark 1. Line 2 baking trays with non-stick baking parchment.

Place the egg whites a large bowl and, using an electric mixer, beat until soft peaks form.
Gradually add the sugar, a little at a time, beating well between each addition until thick and glossy.
Fold through the white vinegar. Using a large spatula, put half of the mixture onto 1 prepared
baking tray and form into a disc shape, making a small nest in the centre for the cream and fruit.
Repeat with the rest of the mixture and place on the second lined baking tray. Bake for 1 hour 40 minutes,
or until a skewer inserted into the centre comes out clean. Turn off the oven and leave the pavlovas
to cool in the oven for 1–2 hours. Do not open the door until the oven has completely cooled.

Meanwhile, prepare the fruit and set aside until ready to use.

When ready to serve whip the cream until medium peaks form.
Spread three-quarters of the cream over one of the discs and top with three-quarters of
the passion fruit and mango. Place the second disc on top of the cream and mango and repeat
with the rest of the cream and fruit. Decorate with fresh mint leaves.

Pimms Punch

The perfect street party wouldn't be right without some classic Pimms to bring out the sunshine. What more can one say, other than "Anyone for Pimms?"

1 part Pimms ✸ 3 parts chilled lemonade
a few mint sprigs ✸ slices of refreshing cucumber and orange ✸ a few luscious strawberries, cut in half

Take a jug (pitcher) or long tall drinking glass, fill with ice and add the ingredients in the suggested quantities. Serve immediately.

Acknowledgements

"I am thankful for the mess to clean up after a party because it means I have been surrounded by friends." Nancie J. Carmody

Thank you, thank you, thank you…

I have really great parents who are rather amazing – in different ways they have enabled me to do everything I have ever wished to do. Dazzler, who is naughty, but truly loved, is so brilliant at what he is brilliant at. My darling daughter Ralphine, the best baby in the whole wide world (who will just have to have the most amazing birthday parties). Millie, who is so kind, and Hope, so brilliantly entertaining – you are the best sisters to Ralphine.

For those I will never forget: days out with Joy, London with Bernard, lunchtimes with Grannie.

Friends are a most important ingredient in this recipe of life, so, to my best friends – we know we are going to be friends forever, our hearts tell us so. Thank you for attending the parties that I invite you to.

Ms Anna Sharp, for being the feather in our fascinator. Miss Tara Staunton and her wholehearted dedication – some people dream of success … while others wake up and work hard at it.

My Pear Tree Family. I thought I was all alone… until I opened the door…! THANKS for being there, 365 days of the year!

Ladies of the book: Emily, Xenia, Ola and Natasha – the ingredients to fabulousness, our journey will be treasured forever in the pages of this book.

Mark Holdstock and Jay Visciano – Bourne & Hollingsworth. Thank you much more than I can say, because you were thoughtful, and made a dream come true.

Introducing you to the Charleston … Miss Kim-Lin Hooper (for more info see: www.charlestondance.co.uk). For shaking and stirring the cocktails, Mr Will Stafford. For sunshine, Miss Alex West. Miss Kitty Verity the camera loves you baby! Miss Emma Gwynne, for your super grin. Miss Zoe Scott, for rose-kissed raspberry jam. A champagne toast to you all!

PICTURE CREDITS ©: pp.4, 5: Lulu Gwynne; 21, 24, 48: Mary Evans Picture Library; 66t: Bettmann/Corbis; 66b: Popperfoto/Getty Images; 89: Lordprice Collection/Alamy; 123: Hulton-Deutsch Collection/Corbis; 124: SSPL/NMeM/Kodak Collection/Getty Images. *Backgrounds:* Cover edge, p.86: The Art Archive/Alamy; 1, 2–3, 4, 7, 8–9, 10–11, 12–13, 14–15, 64: V&A Images/Alamy; 18–19, 20–21, 104: PoodlesRock/Corbis; 16-17, 122: Ben Nicholson/Alamy; 22: Wonderstock/Alamy; 46: National Trust Photolibrary/Alamy.

First published in the United Kingdom in 2012 by
PAVILION BOOKS
10 Southcombe Street, London W14 0RA
An imprint of Anova Books Company Ltd

Text © Lulu Gwynne, 2012
Design and layout © Anova Books, 2012
Photography © Anova Books, 2012,
except those images listed in Picture credits below.

The moral right of the author has been asserted.

All rights reserved. No part of this publication may be reproduced, stored in a retrieval system, or transmitted in any form or by any means electronic, mechanical, photocopying, recording or otherwise, without the prior written permission of the copyright owner.

Commissioning editor: Emily Preece-Morrison
Designers: Georgina Hewitt and Sophie Martin
Photographer: Ola O. Smit
Food stylist/Recipe developer: Xenia von Oswald
Hair and make-up: Natasha at Pretty Me Vintage
Models: Zoe Scott; Charlotte Selby; Jonathan Stickland; Kim-Lin Hooper; Will Stafford; Natalia; Viola; Isabel, Tom & Imogen Haynes; Kitty Verity; Alex West; Emma Robinson, Amelia Holmwood, Liam Currivan, Aaron Millard, Amy Tripp

ISBN: 978 1 86205 973 3

A CIP catalogue record for this book is available from the British Library.

Colour reproduction by Mission Productions Ltd, Hong Kong
Printed and bound by Toppan Leefung Printing Ltd., China

www.anovabooks.com

10 9 8 7 6 5 4 3 2 1